INFORMATION DESK

An Epic

INFORMATION DESK

An Epic

ROBYN SCHIFF

PENGUIN POETS

PENGUIN BOOKS
An imprint of Penguin Random House LLC
penguinrandomhouse.com

Pages 124–125 constitute an extension of this copyright page.

LIBRARY OF CONGRESS CATALOGING-IN-PUBLICATION DATA
Names: Schiff, Robyn, author.
Title: Information desk : an epic / Robyn Schiff.
Description: New York : Penguin Books, [2023] | Series: Penguin poets |
Includes bibliographical references.
Identifiers: LCCN 2022059943 (print) | LCCN 2022059944 (ebook) |
ISBN 9780143136804 (paperback) | ISBN 9780525508311 (ebook)
Subjects: LCGFT: Poetry.
Classification: LCC PS3619.C365 I54 2023 (print) | LCC PS3619.C365 (ebook) |
DDC 811/.6—dc23/eng/20221216
LC record available at https://lccn.loc.gov/2022059943
LC ebook record available at https://lccn.loc.gov/2022059944

Printed in the United States of America
3rd Printing

Set in Warnock Pro with DIN Next LT Pro
Designed by Sabrina Bowers

In memory of my father,
Abraham Harry Schiff

CONTENTS

INFORMATION DESK

An Epic

TO THE JEWEL WASP

When the American cockroach lands
on its back trying to
flick the glorious
wasp off that moves like the hybrid of green tin
and blue glass, gem-
tragic cerulean

task, finite and fathomable as
a photoshopped sea, the
plan is already
in full swing: into the neurotransmitter-
primeval that
drives the bidding of the

now-upended resolute legs of
cockroach American—
six times the size of
the wasp, and the color of a bottle of
Budweiser—thrusts
the neurosurgical

stinger, the accuracy of which
is neither hate nor love
but the beginning
of the brief paralysis in which she needs
to suspend the
roach so, unimpeded,

she can target a second cockroach
ground zero in its roach-
ancient cockroach head.

Do not fear mystery over precision.
That's the mistake
of children in bed whose

abstract suspicions are dismissed. There
was a jewel. Its name
is wasp. She flies off
now to construct a specific nest. Do you
think the roach is
dead? There it stands doing

nothing when the wasp returns drained
from stinging, which you know
kills dead the honey
bees you dreamed of as a girl that prompted you
to pose your first
questions to self as to

sacrifice and valor—and so
weary now, drags herself
toward the roach, who makes
no move to defend itself, and bites off just
one of the crisp
antennae who among

us has not been queried by—as
I was once from a crack
in a cabinet
in a kitchen I was sharing with a friend
whose ex I should
not have slept with. Well, that

was unexpected. I haven't
thought that trespass through in
a long time. Poems

are as good a place for the past as the grass
is for the wasp,
whose iridescent face

shines as she snaps the antenna
off the cockroach and laps
up the blood drink like
the wasp goddess taught her in the vision whose
street name, instinct,
oversimplifies how

satisfying I'm finding it
to say "cock" as often
as I have had the
occasion to here; "American cock," in
particular.
I have good instincts. I

always have. People never shock
me, but I love to be
taken by surprise
by loyalty and candor. How I want the
wasp to mount and
ride the American

cockroach now, but it will have to
do to see the wasp use
the one antenna
the roach has left as a rein to steer it to
the nest she made
it, as a dutiful

stallion of apocalypse is
gently led back to its
stall in hell. Yes, it

will have to do, for now, having soul-hacked the
American
cockroach with a sting to

the brain so precise as to make
the roach stop roach-iden-
tifying and give
itself, body and force, zombie host to the
wasp egg the wasp
is laying inside it,

siblingless, starving-born hatchling
emerging in a few
weeks' time by eating
itself out of the moist gut of the living
roach, who was led,
as I said, not ridden

by the wasp—no riding crop, no
matriarch giddyup,
just a groom and a
walk, and a nest and an egg, and a roach called
cock. It is, it
is, it is enough, but

this is evolution and we've
already come this far.

1

The *Monument to Balzac* might
    be a monument to Balzac
jerking off, and there it stands
    on my roof at all times, invisible
to the human eye,
    but the morning sun casts

its shadow on the front lawn nevertheless
    over the tremendous, morose hostas
that won't die,
    making the day's first shade that makes
my shade garden thrive,
    head jutting in arrogant

ecstasy at its famously
    offensive angle
out of the green slab of the great dressing gown
    he wrote in, beneath
which, in public privacy, his greater-than-
    life-size hands mound

higher and higher,
    holding himself erect on the
hot, black roof eight, twelve, fifteen hours a day at
    solstice as the summer sun climbs and Balzac's pressing
shadow comes
    to preside

lengthwise, widthwise, unrelenting and
    unrelieved, more policy
than judgment,

in obstructionist,
categorical self-regarding,
    absolute dismissal of me over the

whole house and grounds in which I commit this
    observation to these words, now. Does
this shade disturb you as much as it does
    me? Or perhaps you are so
repulsed by the
    words "house and

grounds" I used to
    describe the material
world that the forever panting
    ekphrastic erotic forever self-
satisfying shadow *Monument*
    to Balzac is throwing

is itself so overshadowed
    by the *House Beautiful–*
Guns & Ammo–Elle Decor
    antisocial aspirational vocabulary
I picked up like the clap
    as the former

lowest-ranking telemarketer of
    aggressively inspirational lifestyle magazines
that the fact
    of the monument
I live under is nothing. My
    husband, who is

downstairs today reading
    Portnoy's Complaint,
suggests the shadow has its origin

in the chimney. Guests concur. But passing
under that abject shape in soulful
    loops of mindful

procrastination
    I have witnessed the nuance of its imposition
incarnate as gradually as Steichen must have
    seen it burn into
being in his darkroom—
    collar,

brow, aggrandizing chin—
    after photographing it at 4 a.m.
in the moonlit
    desolation of
magnificent realism, as close to
    abstraction as a stele comes to

the grave it
    marks, rising self-possessed
a gorgeous grotesque instantiation of
    unconditional
loss.
    I used to man the Information Desk in the center of the Great Hall

of the Metropolitan Museum of Art.
    Bull's-eye of that octagon
was an immense urn of flowers
    arranged in silence by florists on
multiple ladders
    each Monday

when the Museum was closed,
    reminding us
that art is mourning. The week descended

on a continuum of scent
from bud to rot
    as the gaping lilies dilated beyond

comprehension, the center of the center of the
    center, wrenched
open for business
    by the force
of time. By late Sunday you could stare right into
    the carpels of those hybrids, called

"Big Brother Lilies" in garden
    catalogs,
into the past of the
    future, which is the same as the past of the present,
but also contains the very moment
    of looking, as

a mirror does,
    and a little more—just how much I don't know,
but might express
    the warp of recalling the future in the past
by here inscribing: "I   knew   you   would."
    Tuesday mornings

the pollen
    was so vibrant my dress was sometimes
marked by it when I walked past
    inside the Information Desk.
The anther rocked on the long filament,
    trembled in communion with

the Calder stirring way upstairs,
    making me aware of
faint currents of air within

the apparent stasis. Not long before
working there, at an
    exhibition of Greek gold, I

circled a thinly beaten oak leaf wreath
    with a golden wasp and two gold cicadas because
my footsteps shook
    the leaves
a little, as in nature, though these were
    under glass. It was

the most beautiful thing I'd ever seen,
    having an impact on an
artifact like that. Vibrating it.
    Playing it.
The gold was extracted
    by way of a mining technique called

"hushing," whereby aqueducts of gushing water
    exposed veins of gold
by sluicing away the overburden;
    my memory rushes
down the artifice
    thus. On my journey from

the Cashier's Office
    to the Information Desk
with a pouch of cash,
    I daily passed Edward Steichen's
elemental photograph of the ghost of Balzac
    honoring the moonlight

before passing the *Final
    Study* of that *Monument*
in a faraway gallery,

followed by Rodin's earlier study of the author,
elsewhere, naked,
    steadied by his

own isosceles
    penis,
which is the negative space between his legs
    and reaches all the way down to the
circular base he stands on as if
    straddling a sundial. Had

I even read Balzac's *Lily of the Valley* yet?
    His favorite of his own
novels? No. But the attar of the lily
    of the Desk
is bound up in my memory
    of those years

organizing
    the money drawer in a black plastic tray, zipping
the cashier's gray money pouch
    back up, signing my name
and so the day begins.
    A guard unlocks a row of doors, crowds

enter, and I am information,
    not so much behind as within the Desk,
a property of the fact
    of the collection, and catechism
commences: *Where's the bathroom?*
    Where's

the bathroom? Can you direct me to a
    men's room? To the Elgin Marbles? Is there a

bag check? Who's your
    daddy? Are those your real
breasts? Why is there an entry fee? What is
    a "suggestion"?
Am I not a taxpayer? Where's the bathroom?
    A payer of
state and city taxes? Am I not a slayer of
    men, same as Napoleon
who stole the
    needle erected just
behind us
    called Cleopatra's (a
misnomer, and obtained
    diplomatically)
in the city's public grass?
    One just like it sits in the path Marie Antoinette was led down to

be beheaded. "Wayfaring"
    is what we call moving
visitors through the building.
    A giant pink condom was once lowered down
upon it. London, sir. The Parthenon Marbles
    are in

London,
    but there's a scale model of the Parthenon
and a model of a fragment of the
    head of a Parthenon horse
in the basement;
    everywhere willful horsemen in misery striving

toward something, away from something else,
    and a horse head
implicit in every bed
    I've slept in. At first it surprised me that

even more than by
    the artwork all around me that

I prayed to, whispered to, studied, and still dream of,
    I was touched by
the man who hired me, and then by his intern,
    who told me once in tandem that
what two gay men do
    to a girl

in public privacy, below the Desk,
    while she is mapping
a tourist's route from here
    to the Temple of Dendur—which before
being relocated to this
    gallery in this

Museum was already
    submerged in water and
scheduled to disappear entirely—isn't
    sexual, nor is it harassment.
There is no word for it;
    so it isn't

happening. What's lost is lost. There was a cart
    we used to transport brochures
from a storage closet
    to the Desk. You had to steer it
back through the Renaissance
    into a passage that

opened in a dark medieval hallway
    through a door without a handle
you backed into after opening
    one-handed with a key called

the "Number Two" that was
        hanging from a

ball-link chain around your neck. We
        talk a lot about death,
my husband and I. I want to add to
        the utter absence
of the weight that once seemed everlasting
        of the child asleep

upon me that
        I can feel not feeling,
which is the overtaking void circumscribed exactly,
        the pressure at my nape
of that ball-link chain when I
        bent down to insert the key

and turn it pushing the door open,
        and the glimmering, insignificant beauty
of the release
        of my neck as I withdrew key from lock,
stood up, and entered.
        My mother swam in

a man-made body called the Delta Reservoir
        near the Mohawk River
outside Rome, New York,
        that was the intentional result of
the engineered flooding of
        a village called

Delta
        that had been developed
into something more than just
        acreage by two men named Stark and Prosper.

You are an American Girl. Here you are in
    an American Poem

getting in the American
    Water. Let's go under
together. "I used to get
    nosebleeds from the pressure. I don't know
that I want to get in the poem—"
    There is a ladder.

Itself a salvage.
    Let's back down it slowly
deep in the quiet American
    Wing of the Museum
in darkness toward a new closet—not for storage
    but installed for public

viewing, a woman's
    wardrobe. Private,
folded things, ironed, crisp
    as peeling an orange in sunlight. Lit
like a refrigerator in a dream,
    with almost nothing in it, who can

stand before it and not
    divest?
Stark and Prosper. Starched and Proper. Stiff and Angry. Forced and entered.
    Sorted and counted. Stored and forgotten.
A pull to bottom I
    associate

with dream ending before
    awakening. Not "thoughtless";
beyond thinking. End-of-recording
    sound of the needle

dragging the void. Why should I, we, be
    afraid? Human consciousness far

predates me
    oiling the mahogany handrail
with my mere presence. *Rembrandt/*
    Not Rembrandt,
1995, was the first special exhibition
    I attended as Museum

employee; paced it with the proprietary edge
    of a paid informant. Submit
everything to the binary.
    It had the stiff, infrared soul
of connoisseurship;
    Rembrandt/

Not Rembrandt, that's the question;
    posed it like a strobe
with the typesetter's solidus, the
    forward slash, a force field between
who did and who did not make it,
    without that indecisive

human "Or" Milton imposes
    between the given and the made—
Eve withdrawing from Adam
    With such gardening tools as art yet rude,
guiltless of fire, had formed, or *angels brought.*
    Choose

a side, poet, which is it—Eve or God
    who forged the hoe? Forgery, forgery,
forgery, flash, flash, flash. I said to myself,
    If you have to ask . . . ,

but I stood before each
    painting

eating half-shadow, umber, and ocher
    every day for a month
of lunch hours trying to know. "The handling
    of the built-up impasto
is itself a valid argument
    against,"

writes the curator, Walter Liedtke, in the
    exhibition catalog,
        <FORGERY>
    and yet, a few paintings over—*Portrait
of a Man ("The Auctioneer")*—"it is
    surprising how

successful the unknown
    painter was
in imitating Rembrandt's manner
    in the light effects on the sitter's
left cuff. . . ." And so I came to love that
    cuff, its lace and dust, and loved the

wrist that cuff suggests, obscured here in the painting
    by the ledger
the auctioneer is holding
    on which the trembling value of what?—some cows?—
suggests a field, in mind,
    where a calf moves

in the shadow of a barn.
    The hot smell of manure
and mulch. A bull. How much is it all worth?
    Self-portrait of the young artist as

auctioneer with your checklist and radiant
    left

cuff that Rembrandt couldn't have
    better lit, I see you; I think I touched that cuff and more
at a keg party in Slonim Woods
    and sensed
its tragic aptitude,
    counterpart to your dull right

wrist
    lacking the vision of an artist's truth. Is that
the word? "Truth"?
    Follower of Rembrandt,
I followed you into the blue woods, but I changed my mind.
    There was a Museum guard who would

not leave me alone in the *Rembrandt/*
    Not Rembrandt
show. Like everyone,
    he used his breaks to flip through
the large black binder of better jobs
    Human Resources left out on a table

for us, and was eventually transferred
    to the Department of Design to
walk the collection with a power drill
    tightening the Lucite fixtures
that held brochures.
    He was

peculiar, and I was afraid of him.
    When he asked if he could sit beside me
in the employees' cafeteria,
    situated down a

private-access stairway
    beneath

the small-scale models
    of a prosperous and tedious imagined
hereafter of a Middle Kingdom
    civil servant served by
a labor force of affectless
    miniature

ghosts trapped
    in menial afterlives on boats, in gardens,
slaughterhouses, cattle stables,
    and a cramped granary
divided into two tight rooms separating
    those hoisting sacks

from scribal clerks squatting on the granary floor
    recording each ounce of grain,
I could not find my no. So down he put
    his tray and we talked awhile.
He did something
    obscene, I

don't remember what,
    with a red cherry tomato. Two months later
he was led out
    of the Museum in cuffs on a date
rape charge, which seemed so new then,
    but as a phrase was coined in

1973,
    so technically is as old as
me. We grew up together
    in the semifinished basements

of the suburbs
    listening to the upstairs plumbing rush the

shit of our fathers
    into the earth. *Rembrandt/*
Not Rembrandt was a show about the audacity of
    no. It either is or it isn't. Rembrandt
or not. But we both know,
    though I

have to say it, there can
    be truth without vision—call it
competence; you follow it out onto the ice
    with confidence
finding purchase on the surface
    in the boot-ruts left by

others, but it will never
    get me across
a lake this size. My mother, a teenager,
    more than half a century ago
on the telephone with a friend on
    a day like this—

crystalline, indifferent—heard his
    little brother through the black receiver
run panting into the house
    yelling that a littler sister yet
had broken through.
    The ice was a

figure when I started that thought,
    but it transformed to ground,
which is the beginning of disaster,
    as ground gives

way to the natural transitions of
    the states of matter, in this

case, just above the solidus,
    the temperature below which
a given substance—lake water, or my will—
    is solid. As a mark
of punctuation— / —
    "solidus" descends toward

us from the
    imperial Roman coin of
(nearly) solid gold, also called a solidus,
    on the same downward-spiraling staircase
that brings "sold" to "soldier"—one who serves
    for pay.

Such coins are on
    display today in Gallery three-oh-one
right outside the gift shop, but a debossed glass weight
    one could use to gauge debasement
is too far away
    to help debate

the worth. *Did you
    consent in basements? Yes/no. Circle one.*
I didn't no.   *And under the Information
    Desk? Did you no?* I would
now. But I didn't how
    so long ago. Rembrandt,

Rembrandt, Rembrandt, not,
    not, not. From slurry to slip
and back we go. Stand up, visitor. This is your hour.
    Here is your map.

Choose your cradle. Ancient Egypt to
    the right. Ancient Greece to

the left as the crow flies, if the crow flew,
    but construction obstructs
its course so you'll see it
    strutting around, lost, making self-important caws
at the temporary walls
    of empire.

What do I mean, "crow"? The boy from SVA?
    The tourist? The teacher? The dramaturge?
Schoolgirl to whom the world has given such
    a small skirt and such a tall
cold stool? Who
    converges

in the Great Hall with me today? Sometimes
    I worked the lines
handing out floor plans
    just to get out from inside
the fact, but Information is a movable
    Desk. John F. Kennedy

Jr. asked me late one afternoon, "What time is it?"
    and I had to tell him, "Not much left
now"; we were
    closing soon. He stood
there throbbing
    like a metaphor. Son of the twentieth

century whose vehicle
    was powered by props.
The Great Poet once admonished me,
    "You are reducing history to anecdote."

"That's more than you ever did!
    Stop raising it

up to myth!" I would have liked to have stood in front
    of *Washington Crossing the Delaware*
holding John-John by the hand
    and told him
I once saw it carved
    in a grain of rice.

Afterward I'd tuck that Stoic
    in eighty yards of wine-dark imported
European textile in the low,
    down bed in Gallery seven-
oh-nine, salute
    good night Medieval

America, and close the high-post
    night curtain. In this / lucid / state of /
poem, / I ad / mit I'm / having / trouble /
    envi / sioning / the age / of
John-John. Mother or
    liaison; boy

or man. Thomas Hart whose bed we're
    in arrived on this land on a ship named
Desire. Who would identify
    with the mother country or
dour country mother
    variety of

Massachusetts witch, living
    apron she who used her hands to wipe her
hands on, practical Ipswich wife to whom
    this bed was left,

in this home,
    willed father-to-son, out from under her?

Lying on the bed
    I can feel the room's dependency, its depth,
a percussive
    loyalty stomping out a fire. And with
a little reach I can use my foot
    to twitch the awful

oaken four-centuries-old cradle situated
    beside me. Imagine
the oak tree overcoming the acorn-tragic
    hunger hoarded by
a rodent.
    Every tree is an

exception. The sturdy wood
    has the self-regarding gloss
of old cabinetry turned
    in anger,
contrived squarely in defiance, in the proportions
    of a coffin; worse, this so-called

cradle
    has a hood that leans a shadow
on the empty.
    Every child thrives at the expense of someone
else's. Though this is just a poem on the
    subject of exhibition—a

double-blind
    protection from statistics—here
I sing to John-John inside the cradle
    inside this primary period inside

the period rooms inside
    the American

Wing inside this Museum. I am mothering a small man/
    wifing a tremendous potential
child/ ovulating in the period room
    and full of it:
Lust. Avarice.
    Spite.

Destiny. Dynasty. Lice.
    John-John John Kennedy Jr. wants to know
what time it is!
    That's the twentieth century behind you, child man.
You can hide inside my skirt,
    but it's

a mini. What's coming's coming for you
    from the sky.
There's a luminous noonday shine
    on the Information Desk
but it's artifice: the Trustees' Dining Room
    glows above like an

expensive, minor afterlife.
    This morning I awoke to pounding deluge—
a furious heavenly manual type-
    type-typing
outside my window that turned out
    to be just

ice on the roof thawing
    but I still call that rain, if from a lower
ceiling than I thought, and I can lower
    my thinking yet,

to the Museum subbasement
    where rats mount a

rotating permanent exhibition
    of excrement
among the white marble B-side nudes and
    dated marble satyrs
that may or may not
    ever see restoration or be seen

above again.
    On the same topic of being,
"Wash me"
    in the dust on the back fender of a moving car
is a traveling exhibition, and of the several ways a tree
    disperses seed

including: by wind drift as an arrow or parachute or powder;
    germinating afloat
upon water
    in pockets of air
like naturally occurring
    versions of the

pontoons that land the De Havilland Otter,
    ready to root
riverside
    where
the river takes them; clinging in infested feathers and matted
    or glossy or soft or not soft fur

with the sad, dignified,
    freeloading no-regret
barbs that inspired
    the marvels of Velcro; ground under the hooves and paws

of anything that charges,
    burrows, claws, herds, stampedes, is

led, leaps, or wanders
    alone across or through or around rivers and ponds,
woods, fields and yellow acreage;
    Dickensian or like
wired-martyrs, self-
    detonating "in circumstances

beyond
    the limits of acceptable fiction,"
and then dispersed further, as in the case
    of common dog violet, whose small shrapnel
gets scavenged by ants who spread it
    incredible

relative distances
    away from the places the seedpods exploded
by dropping a few here and here en route
    to their hills, blazing
the earth
    in inadvertent pathways of dog

violet further
    inadvertently ongoingly dividing
through I don't know how many ages
    of home-going delegates of I don't know
how many
    ants; by the hoarding,

aforementioned, of acorns
    by rodents or jays who are hunted
by predators, or by the scattering
    of acorns

by my son and his friends
　　in circumstances that sometimes shock

me, send me running outside to ask them
　　to calm down, play gently, respect
one another as girls seem to—
　　though my sister and I were certainly
cruel to
　　each other and sometimes

strategic, when we played with acorns
　　play had to do with dolls serving
dolls from beautiful earthenware
　　Art Nouveau game dishes
fabricated in the acorn shape
　　of acorns, and

was never just
　　play with acorns themselves; some birds
in the thrush family
　　eat a kind of vivid berry
encapsulating a tiny adamantine
　　seedcase requiring

a hard-grinding gizzard
　　to wear it down and passes through
the mill of the thrush
　　as through history
belittled, belittled, and belittled
　　until belittlement is the freedom

awakening each seed in shit
　　in the alert procreative natural state
of revenge by which we will
　　outnumber you;

time is the best maneuver.
    No better craftsman than

the clock inside heather,
    a seeding that insinuates into the future
by investing in soil
    and being turned on
by the temperature
    of fire rolling above the moors

like a hell-bent
    plow. Overwhelming
undergoing, what infrastructure shifts
    under this one?
When I slowly crossed the park after work at the
    Information Desk my compass was

the Dakota where Polanski shot
    the exteriors of *Rosemary's*
Baby, but the interiors were shot brightly
    inside my head. Everything
is systems,
    the artist said

at dinner
    describing how FedEx was
initially a cover for the delivery of
    heroin. She told me
about a wind that blows through a Balzac
    novel touching

everyone, even the dead
    slung upside down
in a butcher shop, but couldn't
    remember the title

which led in the trickling manner of dinner
    conversation between strangers

round the same mahogany
    table I had
just breathlessly discovered in a June
    Jordan poem in the Yaddo library
that very morning
    to a consideration

of the size of the penis Rodin
    had cast under
Balzac's cloak.
    Someone said Balzac
had been insulted by the understatement,
    but I pointed out

in the way I had been raised to only
    ever very gently adjust a gentleman,
Balzac was dead when Rodin undertook him
    and you're confusing, I think, maybe Balzac's

with a precedent-setting adjudication
    of a different libeled penis?
The Jordan poem was about a European chewing a peach
    with his mouth open. The man

next to me was complaining about the smell of manure wafting
    into the windows at another artists' colony
that also raised sheep. We weren't really talking about flesh,

but art history, and I'd thought all week
    about whether or not to write the fact of
the writing of this on retreat
    into this poem. True

I sometimes
     do prefer the making

of more than the movie but I don't think
     the making of the making of—
though I love Fabergé eggs,
     etymology,
provenance, evolution, entomology, and long walks and
     don't like to

have to choose between them.
     Manure, maneuver, outmaneuver, manipulation
in the manor, also of artists in
     court.
When someone tells me he's inspired
     I usually take

it to mean someone else
     does his dishes, laundry,
or at the very least cleans under the couch
     where the muses visit him
disguised as students. Confused
     museumgoers sometimes asked, "Where

are the dinosaurs?" Depending on my mood:
     "Across the park, not
far away" or "That's a good question,
     they used to be
right here." Acorn is the
     fruit of the unenclosed land by way

of the same root that gives us our
     acre; God's is the graveyard.
But to whom or what does the oak cradle belong?
     Some say it's the babies', others that we're

only temporary
    stewards

of anything—as my teacher put it, "Who's *not*
    renting his boat?" of the craft Elizabeth
Bishop was seated in in "The Fish,"
    and which I've extended to mean
the borrowed bark
    Wordsworth was rowing

—that doesn't seem to belong to anyone—
    in strokes of regular meter when
overcome by Dread. Death.
    To appalling extent
stewardship is also
    the entitlement with which

eight-year-old Roy Fairchild
    claims, "It's as much mine as anybody's,"
when asked by Laura
    in *Delta Wedding*,
"Is that your boat?"
    Colonialism and the whole undertaking

in a hull. The swagger of him,
    spitting and peeing off the edge
of the commandeered skiff—
    that's not in the book—but you know
this kid. I have an eight-year-old.
    Little shits like Roy grow

up on playgrounds peeling off their shirts and
    stuffing them into their waistbands
where they catch the breeze like dirty
    flags of American boyhood,

cocky Winslow Homer bullies
   seeding the seats

of the classroom
   with thumbtacks,
who dare one another to eat live fish;
   whitewash each other's aunts' nine-foot
fences; and invented a game called "snap the whip,"
   in which a grinning row of bare-

foot princes of Americana
   link hands in embodiment of an eponymous
living whip that ripples
   up the playground
sacrificing its
   outermost segments like the

downsizing,
   autotomizing worms
that inspire collective corporate
   layoffs, the cast-off heirs of which
are right now climbing up
   the ladle-sides of playground slides all over

America
   while smaller boys
are sliding down them. "Released from their lessons,"
   so says the exhibition, "exuberant barefoot boys
engage in a spirited
   game of snap the whip

which required teamwork, strength, and calculation—
   all-important skills for a reuniting country."
For "teamwork," say "collusion,"
   and what a lavish scorn, "exuberance,"

that drives
　　these pale

postbellum punks, whose mothers are still crying
　　over their older brothers' war-dead bodies,
to take the field eight across like a row of
　　chessboard thugs
in formation of
　　an advancing line they named

a "whip"
　　in the name of domination over
every animal and human, including one another
　　and themselves.
Familiar interaction
　　between the sons of men who meet

in orders whose members are said
　　to proudly perpetuate
a myth that each will tie the brick he has been
　　carrying around to symbolize
the weight of tradition
　　to his own penis

with a length of twine cut a few feet longer
　　than the height of the house
he'll be standing on
　　when asked to drop the brick off
in the spirit of belonging
　　on the count of three;

who belong to that house for life, and after;
　　whose children
are their tentacles; and who
　　can reach anything

from anywhere with the right network
    of strings and penises and rooftops and

bricks; and whose cradles,
    which I have studied closely
in person, and books, and rocked
    with my foot in guided meditations slowly in which
I am rock-a-bye wind
    through the branches of oak

from which the very cradle was hewn,
    belong to the still-rectilinear early
early baroque period
    marked by the restoration to the throne
of Charles II
    who'd been

exiled in the France of Louis XIV
    where he'd been introduced to
Continental tastes
    with Asian influences. The furniture,
even in the colonies as the style
    gradually

reached these shores,
    rises top-heavy as a heron,
precariously on legs turned
    in presumption, accomplished
by new joinery known as dovetailing
    in the reign of William and

Mary. Into whose where in which
    of by on up off on with including
against among during upon despite
    concerning beyond.

TO THE OAK GALL WASP

Something like a wooden pearl, what gall
forms here, irritation's
gemstone on the oak-
leaf-underneath I thought was a berry, seed-
case, or oak-faced
scrotum-like excrescence

the oak tree seemed to make of itself
in extremis involved
with power. For no
reason when we were girls plucking these woodland
BBs from the
branch to flick at the back

fence, about so much unsuspecting
I was mistaken by
dissemination
meticulously more single-minded than
the mere widest
distribution of seed

over the furthest expanse; as I
follow American
history, small and
solitary, intravenously driven
living syringe
mainlined into the green

vein of oak leaf to position with
the earthly pulse of her
otherworldly self-

sufficient piercing ovipositor her
shimmering eggs,
the oak gall wasp is un-

American mother of the year.
Patriotism, meet
parasitism;
a biochemical je ne sais quoi charms the
redirection
of the oak leaf's force to

form a cradle for each minuscule
egg something like the way
our human flesh scabs
over. And not just any oak—oak gall wasps
overtaking
an oak known as your own

are implicit in every acorn,
including the sprouting
one you carried home
rolling slowly around the base of a wet
Dixie cup your
first-grade teacher told you

would, with patience, be as tall as you
one day, and capable
in time of crushing
you in bed, unsentimental consequence
of gravity
which is a consequence

of the curvature of spacetime, but
what isn't? I sold the
house behind which my

son and I once planted such an acorn and
even enclosed
it in a pathetic

ring of prefabricated fencing
I fought counterclockwise
against the coil to
unspool off a metal roll like a robot
fabric bolt to
shield it from the orphan

fawns. If that oak rises still, witness
to the sleep of someone
else's child now through
an underestimated August storm, I
do not know, or
in what health, but if rise

it does, safe in her hyperbaric
chamber, as some athletes
sleep between stages
on the Tour de France, there the gall wasp grows in
my divestment.
Such a fundamental

hunger stirs in the oak gall dark, if
you listen you might hear
her chew her way out
of oak leaf where she incubates encrypted
in her first meal.
Unless—and this is life

on earth, as much a miracle of
drudgery and lust as
you or me or the

gall wasp—another even more strategic
parasitic-
to-the-second-power

brood parasite wasp oak-injects with
finer, more exacting
ovipositor,
a second egg. The two sister together
in the waspworld
prenatal ritual

juices, downloading the vital re-
directed principles
of oak into their
maturing, crackling bodies. You've been to sleep-
overs; girls grow
strong touching each other's

bodies with stories of mutual
incrimination. What
confidence betrayed
then when duplicitous behind her back. To
emerge, as we
learned, wasps chew their exit

through the gall; but in the case of a
hosting wasp, she's compelled
to stop by something
most entomologists do not read enough
Victorian
novels to understand.

Whether social dynamics are more
or less legible to
an outsider, I'm

too far inside the gall to tell, since it was
I who dug the
hole, placed the acorn, shooed

the beast, and waited for the oak to
leaf that the gall wasp could
deposit there her
egg, inspiring thus the oak to cradle it
that a second
wasp could parasitize

the parasite wasp—as is drawn out
over several seasons
of elaborate
outmaneuverings in parish, parlor, and
palace on the
BBC. But this is

an American transition of
power. Don't look away.
I don't want to end
this poem bleeding but the wasp does eat the
wasp, and up through
the top of her head like

the goddess she is, enters the hell-
scape. It's happening now;
it happened. Unless,
that is, through the bedroom window where sleeps the
child of someone
else now, the beautiful

oak I tenderly tended alread-
y crashed.

2

There was a second desk
    to the right of the entrance

well hidden behind a pillar. The principles
    of crowd control
ensure you flow right past
    unless you had
Museum business. Instead of giving
    information, there

we received
    the beautiful bike messengers
who resented us
    for being the slowest reception desk
in New York City. They didn't even flirt with us
    so impatient were they with our

procedure
    of needing to look up and call
the four-digit extension of every
    curator's assistant's assistant
for explicit
    permission to send them into the starving maze

of the Museum with
    a badge they had to sign for
and different map
    than we give to visitors
with directions to one particular bank of elevators
    they could only reach by

locating first a marble table,
    once listed lost
on an inventory in Italy,
    but which had been stored and forgotten
in the vast Museum basement,
    the overlooked undervalued

gift of a duke who,
    having purchased it
from a famous estate sale
    called by the *New York Times*
"a curious revelation of *ennui*,"
    wrote to the Museum's first director, "My dear

General" (rank the director
    claimed "without any supporting evidence"
was "awaiting Abraham Lincoln's
    signature on the night of his
assassination")
    "I shall be happy to

present this to the Museum,
    provided it is willing
to pay the boxing, transport and freight from Paris
    to New York." I told each bike messenger
as I rotated the sign-out book
    toward him,

with its long, mint-green pages
    we hand-drew lines in
with ruler and pencil,
    The elevator you will be riding
up to the executive offices
    is just beyond this marble table

I pointed out for him
     on his map. The cold tabletop
symbolizes the depressing extent
     of the whole universe around which
the twelve signs of the zodiac
     death-loop the marble

rim in low relief. If you can just get close enough,
     below enough the low regard of
the melancholic guards so
     many of
are also artists,
     you'll find the patron's name and sculptor's

chiseled in the raised bow of
     Sagittarius, my child's sign,
the far-flung spreading fire feral lawyer to the animals
     with human eyes. And on the tabletop,
two marble
     children sleep

while a third points up to God or the
     Director's Suite, all
of whom are somehow so much warmer
     than the table they're asleep on
despite being of a piece carved
     of the same slab quarried in

Carrara where Napoleon sent the artist;
     and softer yet, unbearably dangling
in the void over table's edge,
     the lushest curl any mother
ever lingered over
     before

smoothing back,

    which the last director—since been asked to step down but who
had not yet stepped up when I manned the Desk, and whose rise
    I could not
anticipate, let alone
    his drop, but whose dim underground

office in the Textile Center
    I dreamed once was
a subway stop on the number six
    and sauntered through in sleep upstairs
to my seat at the Desk—
    says in pillow-talk voice-over on an in-

house promotional Museum video,
    that the sculptor,
who'd traveled as an adolescent by foot
    through revolution-wet Paris,
must have carved before he
    even began to explore

the depth of this marble. The fall of hair off
    the edge before there was a table, a child,
a pedestal,
    and in that unconceived-of-yet child's hand,
a caliper.
    Messenger, I would just sign

for and myself deliver what
    needs deliverance that's since been replaced
by PDF sent via that
    practical low-level mass-market
telekinesis, email,
    that you've got fastened

here in the material world
    with a brad inside a thick
manila envelope inside
    the mouth of your cross-body
bag that distributes the weight
    of a day's work so lustily across

the bias down your back,
    and which years hence
in Atlanta now, town I
    still don't understand, I feel
Nick adjust the strap of as he kisses me
    and turns down the hall of the corporate mid-rise

"mixed-use" building we're renting a bland
    apartment in, were it not in
violation of long-standing
    Museum policy not to sign for
anything, anything,
    at this desk or that

desk in this or the next
    life because
my signature is informed acceptance
    of gifts the Museum
does not acknowledge; such as
    a painting an artist propped against this Desk once and

then so swiftly fled from
    there's no no fast enough,
which had I signed for
    could be claimed as belonging to the
Metropolitan
    Museum of Art! imagine that! but without my

signature the Museum was permitted,
    even *bound*, to dispose of
with cafeteria waste,
    paper cups, plates, plastic
knives, private notes,
    brochures in English, Arabic, Chinese,

French, Italian, Japanese, Korean,
    Portuguese, Russian,
and Spanish, and double-folded
    paper napkins seared
with the kiss of the Park Avenue
    volunteers I sometimes ate with in

those days before recycling,
    and still drifts on
a barge at the periphery
    of my knowledge.
There was a mouse once behind the Desk
    sick with what my friend Toni guessed was a half-poisoning

that wasn't just
    scurrying around, but jumping on
and off the baseboard. Toni had
    suffered a miserable breakup
but was so kind she packed her ex's clothes up
    and drove him to the station

in her red truck, crying.
    Her next boyfriend
who she never loved
    gave her a sundress she never wore. I did a favor for
a curator and was given
    a chartreuse Korean scarf that came

folded in a wooden box. I didn't
   know it was a favor.
I thought it was my job, but never told my
   boss what I did when informed by the gift
it must have been wrong.
   Milky green silk I

sometimes touch.
   And I still have something else, too. I shouldn't,
but I do. When the guard who followed me
   through the *Rembrandt/Not Rembrandt* exhibition
became a Design Assistant
   he promised and

made good on
   securing me a Sugimoto exhibition poster that was
not for sale.
   One of two hundred seascapes the photographer framed
equal parts sky and water
   over and

over in every sea, over and over, as identical
   to the inattentive as
the horizon seems to the lost. How high
   can you go? I ask my
soul; how low?
   The limitations

of technology once
   made balancing the exposure
of the trembling
   seascape gold with the shivering sky
technically insurmountable so
   Gustave Le Gray, forefather of Sugimoto

whose exhibition poster suggested to me
    from a metal stanchion I could see
from my seat at the Information Desk
    that time and distance
could be traversed
    in the same vehicle without

me even rising from my chair
    and which the Design Assistant
offered me the gift of when the exhibition
    closed and the poster advertising it
was no longer needed,
    created two separate

negatives and printed them in private
    in his red-velvet-draped portrait studio darkroom
together
    as one luminously deepfaked horizon,
even collaging distant coasts
    under

different skies during different
    times of day in single impossible evening
sunrises and moonlit noons
    like photographs of cognitive dissonance,
not in deception, I think,
    but in

realization of a quivering light beheld in nature
    he was otherwise
incapable of holding.
    I didn't want the gift, but I wanted
the poster. In exchange
    all I had to

do was acknowledge
    the favor, and in this hint of gratitude
appear to him
    not followed but
accompanied through the galleries.
    "Illusion and Deception" is chapter 1 of the

two-volume boxed-set catalog of *Rembrandt/Not Rembrandt*
    wherein it's said Rembrandt propped
his painting *Young Girl*
    Leaning on a Window Sill facing outward
down upon the street
    whence from passersby

waved up at it, or her. Much is made of the allure
    of the young girl—servant
or model—whoever she is,
    but of the recess behind her,
that boundless weeping shadow
    like an abject

watercolor made pliable via a cold sweat,
    if you enter that darkness,
you enter alone.
    But, nihilist, don't call that background nothing.
From the vacancy comes tromping
    the grunting,

lowing frequency of the hand-ground,
    hoof-mouth pigment "bone black."
There's a slaughterhouse behind
    us. Bovine; porcine; human? Bone black pigment
is prepared by placing
    bones in a crucible

and depriving them
    of oxygen.
Then you grind the char
    into a baby-powder-fine
denial of soul until it's pure matter
    into which a painter or painter's studio apprentice

adds linseed or walnut oil
    to mix a paint according to the viscosity desired
to repress
    the stable, the sty, the stile, the pasture,
the butcher, the dripping,
    and the odor;

but it all surfaces in the blackest black
    Rembrandt/Not Rembrandt
painting of anyone. See
    how the portrait
hanging upside down from
    a crossbeam, huge, decapitated, extravagantly

illuminated, almost igneous, *Flayed Ox, Side of Beef,*
    so-bright-you-can-almost-
read-by-it
    portrait of the artist as
meat
    looms out of darkness painted with a pigment made of

cooked bone? Background is
    foreground is
background is the bone black
    to which Rembrandt added additional pigment
to embody variation
    stirring the abyss. Back up, visitor. "The smell

of color will bother you," Rembrandt warned
    studio guests away
from his work. Art history explains
    this is how
to micromanage an optimal viewing distance
    wherefrom the eye

can synthesize radiant illusory effects
    into gems, brocade, gold chain, and lace
as rigid as a fence
    which at close range just looks like
the crudely modeled paint it is;
    but we wolves crave

the smell of death; take him at his word;
    can't get close enough. Animal
knowledge drags the brush
    through the grass, the woods, the chase,
the pain, the wild panting paint.
    Of all the pigments Rembrandt combined with stock-

yard bone black including:
    azurite,
envisioned here first
    in honor of NASA's announcement this morning
of the discovery of water
    on the sunlit surface of the moon I just ran

down the stairs to share
    the shimmering news of with
Nick; found him asleep
    on the couch; what day is it?
October 26, 2020, 2 p.m.;
    a blue moon is rising on Halloween,

a few days from today,
     and the day after that, daylight saving ends
marking the beginning of
     the winter period of
the squandering of sacred darkness,
     and next Tuesday, Election

Day in America, as good a time as any
     to confess I don't know what to do
about the fact that the Now I keep
     rising to the surface of
keeps changing
     in the course of this

poem while time courses through me,
     as when
a teenager swimming with friends in an
     unsupervised backyard pool we didn't
skinny-dip nearly enough in but
     into which I plunged once alone through

an aqueous, unforgiving kingdom of light
     that penetrated to
the lowest depths
     I held my breath to madness to behold,
coming up for air I
     knew I would never belong to my

friends again, there on the pool deck, beautiful, tan, laughing
     about something someone said, and then
someone arrives with a cooler of his
     father's beer, and
someone else hands me a towel,
     as if

I am a body;
 smalt,
called "cobalt" when taking the temporary form
 of a bottle on a shelf,
a blue ground glass phase-transitioned from liquid
 after being plunged into ice; ochers and

umbers of the earth
 in cave paintings depicting
among a herd of wild goats, a goat
 on two feet, taut below the pelt of which, a bow I
cannot see, but a microscope reveals
 fretwork in

the baroque exoskeletons of
 phytoplankton
that at one millimeter per century
 over seventy million years built up
soaring vertical chalk deposits
 like the Cliffs of

Dover where chalk is extracted
 and exported
and chemical analysis detects traces of at the bottom of
 an almost intact clay pot
found in a cesspit
 under Rembrandt's house; reds are the

most forsaken—unbearable gash-bright
 vermilion
prepared according with modern Dutch method
 in a "retort," a specialized
bent-neck lab vessel resembling
 the head of a waterbird

in which sulfur
    and cinnabar in its quickliquid
mercurial form
    heat together to a vapor
that crystallizes and gets scraped out
    as in a D&C a deep slaughterhouse red

blazing the huntsmen's coats,
    robes of Saint Jerome,
and the vivid, burning gowns
    of how many tragic, triumphant
inexperienced married widow
    experienced virgin untitled English

French Dutch titled American women, turned out
    at home, in private parks, public halls,
dancing and strolling,
    reclining and standing,
throughout the Museum
    in a time-darkened darkening shade

of volcanic activity
    in oblivious vermilion reluctant acknowledgment
of the Spanish convicts and
    enslaved North Africans
who died extracting it
    from the same mine whence comes

imperceptible trace bleeding
    from an incision in the neck
of a Bronze Age Cycladic figure
    which ultraviolet light
trained like a knife at the jugular
    makes perfectly clear.   Who told

you that
    one paints with emotions?
One makes use of emotions,
    but only paints with material.
                            How
                    I love
                            to touch
                                    this world.
Its cactus spines and parasites—
    its cochineal, from

whose tiny steadfast bodies, born
    starving like all of us,
derives the reddest dread.
    They hatch almost immediately
from a clutch of eggs laid while
    their mother's mouth was stuck inside the host, then

crawl in a fog toward the edge of the cactus
    where by chance the wind catches
their bristles as it does the sails of a galleon
    and distributes them
among nearby cacti where they
    lodge their new

faces into cactus flesh
    and never move again, spending their
whole lives feeding and dreaming I
    don't know what, feeling, if they feel,
the feel of rain and
    ancient dirt and deadly sun and the

intrinsic longings
    of their kind even as they swell

in perpetual fulfillment. Press
    one, like this, between thumb
and forefinger and out comes their one
    self-defense: carminic acid—a foul

humor that turns off in ants
    the instinct to otherwise
eat such easy marks, leaving
    my fingers, though it isn't blood,
looking like I stopped a nosebleed, if I wiped
    across your shirt would remain

colorfast there the luster of bloodthirst
    for the next six centuries,
while other red dyestuffs
    are fugitive. Something of the violence
with which the mouthpart
    of cochineal embeds in cactus

and the lust we share to crush it
    gleams in the red dress
of Rembrandt's *Jewish Bride*,
    its palpable transactional monomaniacal
hunger, same as the red
    of the redcoats who are coming

yet all over everything they
    touch, and the American flag Key would see
in the dawn's early light lording
    it over Fort McHenry. Though he wouldn't
have known it—shriveled, raided,
    traded

dead, listed by the ton on the
    manifests of Spanish fleets

overtaken by privateers and pirates,
    and finally ground to dust by
some Dutchman presuming himself
    grinding dried berries of

"New Spain," the conquest of which is
    inferred in every stroke of red laid by any
Old Master
    liquid enough to buy it—
in the insect-on-its-back quality of flailing limbs
    feeling up the

torso of that bride,
    Rembrandt
recollects in red with so much life
    it hemorrhages,
an infestation. The Design Assistant passed the
    Sugimoto exhibition poster to me over the

Information Desk rolled up Seascape-in
    into a tube he eyed me through
as he crossed the Great Hall
    in the manner of a child pretending to
deploy a telescoping spyglass
    on the deck of

a ship; and rolled up
    it remained in the back corner
of closet after closet—too ashamed to hang
    but not to have it—as I trickled through
the sublets
    of those years. Had it framed finally in

Iowa City, Iowa, and squared it
    1,049 miles west of the Atlantic,

2,032 miles east of the Pacific
    over the toilet
down which Nick once
    flushed a

glistening plastic bag
    of crack I found beside the house
in a prism of light playing off
    the filthy slush in a temporary first
thaw of March.
    At what point in the many years of staring at

that horizon whence from toward which
    did a single beetle—species unknown to me
of which there are 350,000-plus,
    the largest group
of any animal on earth—
    enter that frame

and die there? Whose afterlife is a self-storage unit
    in Atlanta, Georgia,
I just realized I don't
    know where I put the key to,
what would I gain from knowing what
    to call you? My sister sent

me a Chanel lipstick for my birthday
    a shade named "Moment."
It contains the same ingredient
    Queen Elizabeth wore on her lips
in procession to St. Paul's Cathedral
    to give thanks for the

conquest of the Spanish Armada, Color Index 75470,
    God blew

and they were scattered. The detection
    of life in art
is serious. First listen
    for movement, which I

practiced as a girl against the nightly whirring
    in my bedroom walls
my father told me
    was the living music
of my circulation, then take measure
    of carbon dioxide and methane to

determine the presence of
    the respiratory activity of termites,
wood microbes, other insects whose
    spiracle breath puts them
in league with the wind system
    of the organs of Bach. Mere

visual detection
    is impossible in all but the most
dire levels of infestation.
    How long after closing the wooden door
against the darkness at the entrance
    of a rock-cut tomb

hewn in the Middle Kingdom by dying men
    from living rock
did the wasps of antiquity
    begin to pare it down
with their face-drill drill-bit jaws? She masticates
    the pulp in air in flight back to

her nesting site and creates there
    the kind of nest that inspired

the invention of paper
    with just the miracle of her saliva
the more of which this wasp mixes with wood
    the more waterproof

becomes the nest.
    Do you believe in God?
I believe in the elemental
    attunement of wasps.
During the wet year 1996
    as I walked in a blizzard from the Desk down the center

of Fifth Avenue with a friend
    who sold tickets at the entrance
of Ancient Egypt, paper wasp nests assembled
    for study proved thicker with saliva
than nests collected
    in drier years. A

barometer
    is not more
precise. When newly hired,
    I was sent into the galleries with a checklist
to familiarize myself with possessions
    I might be asked by a visitor to point

out on a map or toward which
    I could steer one on one's way toward
something else. The digressions
    are endless. I can get
anywhere from anywhere but had
    trouble locating a barometer I

was finally told was reading the air
    from a gilded wall

beyond a mechanical table
    built for Marie Antoinette to convert
from writing surface
    to makeup desk with the turn of a crank.

A recess below the marquetry
    conceals a mirror released
with the press of a button;
    other buttons open
marquetry panels that turn out
    to be the lids of six hidden com-

partments that held the queen's
    cochineal and vermilion rouge and lipstick and
the lead white face powder that—
    in production for two thousand years,
poisonous and luminous—made
    the crazed whites of that age

crazier and whiter. To compart-
    mentalize; to hide things
even from oneself
    is European expertise as easily
exported to the colonies
    as a cockroach in a shipping

crate. Oak veneered with marquetry of
    mahogany of Honduras; holly,
amaranth, barberry, stained
    sycamore, and green-lacquered
wood; gilt-bronze mounts; steel, iron
    and brass fittings; mirror glass;

and velvet (not original). Insect
    damage to the fabric lining

of a closed compartment
    inside the cabinetry
undermines the integrity of the whole
    just as infestations of

deathwatch beetles,
    deemed repo men
by those who hear the unholy banging
    of their frantic heads against the substrate
from within tables, chairs, and wainscoting,
    underscore the violent sourcing of

imported wood. How to guarantee against
    repossession by the natural world? First
isolate the object
    in a microclimate
that replaces oxygen with
    unbreathable air like

the helium the Declaration of
    Independence is suspended in
at the National Archives
    such that its inside voice
is of a child
    who just huffed the last balloon she brought home from a

party where the eldest brother
    of the birthday boy pinned her down
and spit and sucked
    his slobber back;
then wait for insects to drop from
    the object, dead. Be careful to be thorough. Carcasses provide

nutrition for newcomers who'll
    tunnel through the wood for years

eating hidden networks of dust-filled
    trenches into any wooden object; it will seem
intact but is as nearly hollow
    as so

much poetry. But then
    —this touches me—
the process of restoration
    is to feed a strip
of paper through the channel—thus insect
    damage is filled in with the product of the inspiration

of insect-craft; the mafioso
    whiff of which, such that when the force
protecting you is the same
    you need protection from—
that fundamental essence of
    religion, law, and politics—moves me

so much I would like to handwrite
    a curse or blessing along the paper that's fed
into that void—
    just a simple line,
like dialogue ribboning out of the mouth
    of a saint in the margin of

a book of hours
    to mail into the narrow pass
blasted by the course of
    life that runs inside all things.
But what to write? One day at the Desk it was discovered
    that floor plans that had been altered

by the hand of some artist or vandal
    had been stocked among

our stacks of handouts
    and so were fed into the Visitor
Services office shredder
    one by one, dozens of them. No one who saw

them would tell me what
    was said. Why so discreet,
you who asked me if I was wearing
    a push-up bra as I sat down to work and who
assisted our boss in pulling
    Betsy's skirt down inside the Desk

on the other side of which visitors were
    grabbing our brochures?
What presence, indelible on the folded map,
    silenced you?
I hid a copy of a book I wrote
    behind a basement panel

in a house I sold a few months after
    starting this poem. I'm sorry, Louise and
what's your husband's name?—
    sociologists who bought
my house and kindly without
    judgment forwarded a sweater

to me in Atlanta
    I'd accidentally ordered to my old address,
those on whom now coldly falls the
    shadow of the *Monument to Balzac*
who knew the world
    by describing it object

by object,
    there's something to object to

in the basement, subject to silverfish and roaches,
    I did not disclose
in the disclosures.

TO THE CUCKOO PAPER WASP

The first crisp tool in a small set of
perfect lockpicks this slick
wasp learns how to twist
is time. A solitary operative
whose name honors
the bird famous for its

home invasions; obligate brood and
kleptoparasitic
crafter without craft,
not a papermaker like her makerspace-
industrious
hostess who 3D prints

a many-chambered paper shelter
with her drooling mouthparts,
cuckoo paper wasp
whose patience is a weapon whetted slowly
just waits as the
real paper wasp foundress

spit-forges her nest, killing time late-
lying in her bed of
winter mind-humming
Helter Skelter to the cuckoo paper wasp
eggs depth-charging
within her. Then, prepared

by visions shared by the most poised of
athletes, practitioners
of mental training

who feel their achievements before achieving
them because they
know imagination

is muscle equal to the heart, she
emerges from her long
overwintering
already on the hot prowl; malware's mascot,
she creepy-crawls
the spring wind with her six-

jointed forelegs, watches paper wasp
complete and provision
her nest from a short
distance whence, as if out of swift nowhere, so
oblivious
is the paper wasp and

consequently not en garde against
what she can't imagine,
serves herself as both
eviction notice and quick enforcer, a
conspicuous
example of how those

of us who don't know how to make our
homes make the ones we find
ours, story lines I've
followed alone too many times on hotel
television
scaled back for anodyne

apocalypse programming that the
entire history of
civilization

is the slow-motion dress rehearsal for: she
murders her and
usurps her nest. How? In

place of skill, paper wasp 2.0
honed her face to use as
a club. Pronouns hung
a scrim behind which wasp double-crossed wasp and
her nest became
hers; then she lays further

claim to it by laying her own wasp
eggs there among those the
authentic paper
wasp placed first, each forthcoming life a secret
froth brimming its
neat wasp-paper cell, the

weirdest cupcake batter aquiver
in thin paper liners.
What a terrible
birthday party planned in resentment and guilt
and love. Hard to
grasp in pictures, I climb

a step stool with a flashlight and peer
into the rafters to
see this nest myself
resisting my sister-in-law's demands to
use the broom she's
trying to hand up to

me to sweep it down, and even then
who knows what's what, who's who,
can tell a fatal

cradle from a throne? By now the new queen has
assumed the scent
of the host she killed by

rubbing herself against the nest to
take on the essence of
the paper chewed in
that murdered wasp's small mouth, like dry-bathing in
the parched jaw of
death, a sacred lake bed

whose dust consecrates her in what's called
"chemical camouflage"
by those of us who
think we have the distance not to become the
subjects of this
queen. But who knows? To the

queen the queen is the queen. Deception
and Self-Deception was
a popular course
at the college I attended long ago
that was one of
those mansions before that

built on other people's loss on farm-
land secured by slaughter.
Of the spirit of
the bald eagle, observed more easily in
situ than the
real estate dealings of

wasps, Benjamin Franklin is said to
have said he wished it not
the chosen emblem

of this land. That bald eagle's dishonesty
is bald-faced. You
must have seen one perched high

upon a dead spruce, his visage in
serious profile so
iconic it's like
beholding a living coin transacting the
wild air. There
is an eagle somewhere

on our money, isn't there? I could
swear it but what a long
time since studying
a quarter. Remember the satisfaction
letting go of
one into a slit cut

for it exactly, utterly in
sync with spending power
departing the loud
arcade with one coin left over to phone your
mom? The heft of
the cold receiver and

delve of the coin into a Delphic
cleft in metal where that
eagle descended
to fish—if he fished. Too lazy to hunt for
himself, he trains
his aristocratic

long-range gaze on an osprey fishing
two miles downriver. When
that bird has made his

catch and is bearing it back to the nest to
feed his young our
bird pursues and steals it.

You have seen one perched on a spruce and
known the score. But here in
this paper nest I
can't stop looking at there's no seeing what con
the cuckoo wasp
larvae are pulling to

move the worker paper wasps, emerged
now with no suspicion
that their queen is dead
or that spring said *long live the queen*, to feed them
first, before they
feed their own. That subtle

incompetence a cuckoo paper
wasp is born wielding that
a real paper wasp
responds to with its wasted love is what makes
a cuckoo wasp,
not a papermaker

but maker of the law, a better
choice.

3

Contrary to what
    I once believed to be their near-immortal
constitution,
    deprived of oxygen in an old jam jar,
rounded up body by
    body as they

scrambled under someone's sink
    over the course of
I don't know how many days or weeks
    and brought by coat pocket into
a French period room where the Trustees were
    gathered for dinner behind a

folding screen,
    cockroaches landed DOA in proximity
to the writing desk of Louis XV,
    failing thus
to infiltrate that woodwork, itself an
    imitation of Chinese lacquer—

God's plastic—both the secretion
    of the female
Asian scale insect *Laccifer lacca*,
    named for the Sanskrit word for the swarm of
one hundred thousand of her coating a tree
    in a sumptuous

ectoplasm I would like to
    lick,
and a scarlet resin like it—

thick, deep, sticky, and hard
as the hard candy layer of a candy apple—
    made from the toxic tree sap of a relation

of poison ivy.
    Which is it? Insect or plant?
Who or what? The original black silk velvet blotter
    upon which the king of France unrolled
his map and spread his documented
    mistress was lost

before his giant desk was brought to this
    gallery in the year of my birth.
But matter never disappears
    entirely. I stroke the vestige
of that fabric, chewed up, swallowed,
    metabolized

through the abdomen of silverfish
    and shit-deposited back into earth
where the wild root hairs of an oak tree,
    from which was hewn
this borrowed desk I write this down on,
    groped that desperate

velvet power. *The year of my birth?*
    This very desk?
Endowing me with what self-centered knowledge
    it's my job or fate to disseminate
from the Information Desk? A stranger
    once approached me

there and said,
    "I was on your flight last week!
You were on my plane!"

And so I was. We crossed the Atlantic
together and saw it all from thirty-eight thousand feet
    tracing the same destiny as a

portable silver candleholder
    in Gallery 546 bearing the mark
of its maker: I S, that stood once with
    a stirring view of what's called
the Place de la Concorde,
    now. (My

teacher should have said, *Who's*
    not borrowing his desk?, and so I pass on
to my students.) In the season of the cockroach
    someone made his mark by blade
to what was then considered the work of
    Rembrandt

depicting Jesus, but has been demoted since
    to any pilgrim,
and attributed to
    A Follower. One day you're immortal;
then you're
    in a rented kitchen breaking sheaves of

angel hair pasta
    over a pot that's
much too small for
    it. But at center of the Information Desk
I staff the eye of Time triggering
    the attention of its tears, spit-polishing handrails

with breath of ruin.
    Sometimes on my break
I'd take my name tag off so no one'd know to

ask anything of me—such as on the longest days
of winter break in a slowly chilling
    voice reserved for

when she'd had enough my mother'd
    say, "I'm not your mother"—
and I'd sprawl as she did in our living room
    across the only sofa
in the Museum not
    cordoned off with red arousing rope like

enormous nipple tassels of
    grief and lust and read Balzac's *Lily of the Valley*
under the moony
    portrait of Princesse de Broglie,
an aged descendant of whom, staunch
    with flirtatious guilt, asked

me at the Information Desk
    soon after opening on a day
that wing was closed
    for special permission to see that ancestor
she'd been told she so resembled
    but whom she said she'd only

ever seen in books
    framed above a defunct
mantel regal in a long, cold gown
    the infinite blue
of sorrow and wealth. She is so noble as to have
    four necks: start with the most conspicuous

around which gold shows
    her jugular how to throb,
then take that staircase one flight down

to the throat of her wrist encircled
in a helix of a necklace of so many
      pearls a mere bracelet is of

insufficient breadth to bed the many
      oysters from whose recurring
nightmares out they rolled, down with which we go
      one further lucent turning to ground-level
viewing of the naked
      body who stood

for the Princesse that the artist could,
      with the trademark accuracy of ice,
drape over a true female anatomy
      that killer silk
to gaze into is to want to
      drown yourself. That's three—! then

rush all the way back up the staircase to recall
      in the tremble of her feather hair clip
the retracted neck of the sub-Saharan
      marabou stork in flight—
the "undertaker bird,"
      so called from

behind its back for how much those cloakish wings
      —the largest span of any land bird—
look like a hunched Victorian death-dealing
      a cadaver. Which it is!
Tuberculosis!
      Oh Princesse! Why

don't I feel more for you?
      Your early death, your blue dress everyone
wants to taste, and the restrained sadness

that droops your eyelids
as if you're a little high or hiding
    something big and willing yourself

not to scream. I want to love you, too,
    but I'm too jealous
of how your opera gloves,
    nonchalantly filled with
having just been to the opera, are slung
    over the arm of the chair you're leaning

on to reveal how your elongated
    ungloved fingers taper
into tips so attenuated
    you could pick a different
lock with each
    and simultaneously enter ten different

exclusive realms of being,
    unlimited by time, gravity,
birth, or money. I flew first-class once!
    As we were transcending into oblivion
a rubber-gloved steward
    using a dot-matrix

printout of the manifest to correctly address
    each first-class passenger by name
tipped toward each of us a basket of
    what I thought were credit cards
like a reverse collection plate,
    that turned out

to be individually wrapped
    sanitary wipes
miraculously packaged, slick and glossy, containing

a sheet as elegantly folded
as an insect wing moistened by
     desire of

angels to purify ourselves against the armrests
     and whoever's seated in coach
behind us lulled in neutered chorus
     beneath the white noise of the fans,
acceleration,
     velocity, and

lift. Airspeed,
     altitude, trend, and Mach
are determined via coordination
     of a critical network
of pressure-sensitive instruments
     including an open tube system adapted

from an eighteenth-century French tool developed
     to measure rushing river water
through which airflow is gauged
     in flight, but into which, quickly on
the runway with mud she
     rolled into a globe and

flew here from a nearby puddle,
     a keyhole wasp
sculpts her secret nest. First
     she evaluates potential. Is tube
deep enough to conceal
     her egg? Sufficiently narrow? Night enough to trust the

future to
     emerge through? *Wasp*, so says this hollow,
I am the yes that opens just

for you; I have been gaping
since the beginning of my shape
   enduring the entrance of wind and rain and exhaust

awaiting your investment; thus keyhole wasp
   drops into the shaft a single egg
followed by one
   single slow-breathing
paralyzed grub; then in high literary style
   described by Poe, uses the

mud she gathers to wall them in
   together. Knowing what
we know of privacy and
   hunger, I want to watch this quarantine
tighten around this living theater
   as much as you, but with cabin

door secured, handheld electronics
   switched to airplane mode, and stowed items
overhead beginning their irrevocable
   fated shift, takeoff
commences and the small universe
   of that wasp nest

comes to constitute such
   blockage of airflow through
the tube it's lodged in that
   fatal miscalculations of airspeed
bring the whole craft down. Avert your eyes and think about
   luggage. Things of this world, how

I want to hold and count you.
   Heaps, piles, stocks, troves, drifts, reserves,
reservoirs, packs, pecks, stacks, wagons, freight and

tracks, routes and goods,
dams and locks, the descendant of the Princesse
    is leaning toward me—whose family

still owns those very gloves and shawl and jewels and chair,
    pets them formally
somewhere in Paris in their acid-free storage chamber
    with an air of ritualized
kink, those props
    rendered coolly in paint

as to seem untransformed by art,
    where light fathoms life silk by
leather by flesh by
    feather, invoiced and inventoried
catalog of stalking,
    herding, breaking, breeding, harvesting, hunting, cutting,

plucking,
mining,
exacting,
and importing
that portrait
is—
    reared
over the Desk
    toward me
so she was on the side of Information
    and issued her request.
An easy Yes grants access, but how

to map a route?
    The portrait occupies a point
directly through Medieval Europe
    down a Byzantine corridor

of the sort of domesticities
    carried away in dog mouths—smallest

spice spoons, measuring cups grooved
    with gradations not concerning us,
bracelets, buttons, a single silver hoop earring
    "one of a pair,
the other lost" that
    causes an involuntary response to

reach suddenly for both
    my lobes. My mother says, "Shake out your
sweater gently," and sometimes sure enough;
    but usually what's gone is gone for good.
"If not for Christmas crowds,"
    I told the descendant,

"to reach that portrait
    you'd pass through this choir screen,"
I circled on her floor plan, past an empty doll crib
    once attended to with fear, song, and rocking
by a resentment of devoted sisters
    unlike

those I played with as a girl,
    the pairs of us who'd re-pair off by age
and sister newly in fresh upstairs bedrooms
    flipping on the kind of pull-up bars
you screw into a threshold
    and promise not

to flip on
    while parents gossiped until midnight downstairs,
but the kind of sisters
    beyond play. For games, I'm told

my father had one toy: a shovel he used
     to shovel dog shit into paper bags

he lit on fire on his neighbor's porch.
     All of an August at the boardwalk as a girl
I tried so hard and
     failed to win an invisible dog
you knew was there because
     suspended by transparent

wires its taut red leash
     and muzzle at once described and broke
a presence. Today I play an inherited game
     of shoveling
that dog's powerful invisible excrement
     into Amazon

boxes for distribution among my neighbors.
     It's Christmastime in my
poem, but Prime Day in America,
     coinciding with the summer solstice
that inspires everyone with
     its ancient

associations with fire, fertility,
     hooves, and dust
to order something we don't already have
     such that a handheld vacuum
out for delivery since 7 a.m.
     comes for me through the

humidity and torpor. My mother had
     a favorite doll whose face
melted into toxic mud when she left her
     in the back seat of the family car

on a day like this
    when she was brought to

see moondamp newborn calves
    at a farm en route
to their new life in Rome, New York,
    where her father, a Procurement
Specialist, had been transferred to an installation
    named Griffiss Air Force Base for

an airman shot down by friendly fire
    over the English Channel—
the first American airman killed
    in the European theater of World War II—
designated since
    a Superfund site, and

closed in the course of *Rembrandt/*
    Not Rembrandt while I sat at the Desk,
where PCP, lead,
    multiple solvents used
in the repair, maintenance, and modification
    of aircraft, and stored, shipped, and buried

materials of war and warfare research
    bled into the groundwater
that nurtures absolutely
    with its corrupt love
down into where up by above thoroughly, and
    dirges from the glistening

tap, contaminating as it provisions
    even the generous thinning of
third-day leftovers in a pot on a
    back burner, transferred to

family table via
    a passed-down porcelain

soup tureen we never owned the lid to
    my mother now keeps decommissioned
on a mirrored shelf where
    you can see the depth of its
emptiness. Our one heirloom,
    washed and stocked repeatedly with that

noxious runoff, a blue-and-white
    imitation Meissen Orientalist fantasia
of weeping willows whose boughs droop
    in the white air
like towels hung out
    to dry on a hot overcast day

growing more sodden yet in wet heat,
    and three slow men crossing
each of several identical repeating footbridges
    hold their fishing poles
out in front of them like flags in a parade,
    the tureen

was the settlement of a business debt
    resolved right before leaving The Country
referred to only ever by anyone who fled it
    as "Old." (No, not flags,
just flagpoles with nothing waving.)
    Pressed

upon them rather than *collected*, I hope,
    but no details back me up,
no anecdote at all except
    that there was a lid left behind everyone's

always talking about wishing they
    could put

down on it. What of
    the other family?
The one who settles up
    in porcelain? Who stays in that Country
with no money, presumably no passports? (Not flagpoles—
    broomsticks, truncheons, pitchforks, hatchets . . .)

Churchill called anecdotes
    the gleaming toys of history.
A child then, daughter I guess,
    secreted that lid under her bed
and in the privacy of her theft, rocked her doll in it,
    denied that the

fundamental part of what makes a lid
    a lid was missing, called it whole,
knew the men who drew her out from
    under the bed from town, and also knew
their daughters (hammers, knives, dogs, and bricks).
    My mother

says the hot smell of animal overwhelmed her.
    Rich interior stink of sunlight
coming under the barn door, wet acrimony
    of manure and birth,
straw and mud and milk;
    it makes her sick to

think about the swinging wattle
    of a cockerel carried somewhere in a bucket,
and back in the Dodge parked in dirt,
    facing the sunken doll face

dripping on the backseat.
    "Thank you!" He who rang the

doorbell is nearly back inside his truck
    when I fetch my vacuum from
the front porch. Meanwhile I just
    canceled reservations to sleep
in an Airbnb a few hours' drive from here
    in the Blue Ridge

Mountains the host calls a *European Villa.*
    A picture
of the host taking a picture with a flash
    ignites a tawny torch
in the second bedroom bureau mirror
    situated between

two twin beds, each with a pillow over its face that reads
    Relax
in red stitching.
    "But for Christmas flesh," I told the descendant,
—in whose face, as she leaned into the airspace
    of the Information

Desk, I could see the reconfiguration
    of an honorific royal algorithm
running the data
    of its murderwealth—
I would thread you through this
    interconnecting European

network of period rooms
    to simulate in our immersive
path the experience of being asked
    by your ancestral Princesse

to visit her at home. Winding through
　　this maze of grifts, the gifts

of steel magnates, drug lords,
　　refiners of sugar, and oil men,
in double-backing avenues of crystal,
　　moonstone, gold, and lacquer,
I'd take you past a microscope that stands
　　on a tripod that stands

on the desk of Louis XV the magnification
　　power and craftsmanship of which,
fabricated in gilt
　　bronze, brass, gold tooling, mahogany,
and handblown glass, "qualifies it
　　both as work

of art and working scientific instrument."
　　The shaft is wrapped in sharkskin
the shade of blue stirred green
　　in the depths of the Atlantic
where north waters meet the south;
　　shouldn't there be underwater

thunder where these pressures coalesce?
　　I've seen a shark migration;
multiple species—spinners, blacktips—requiems
　　passing as a single presence as we
watched them from the shore.
　　Undeniable

traffic of intention;
　　sand unionized by their moving bodies
whipped up a graininess
　　like old film to view them

through, so it felt *historic*
  but of course, is not. I've seen a shark migration; but

to hear one, that's another story.
  Undersated ancient rapture;
understated hunger brontide;
  underslung unrumble cut-the-engine inner
silence thrash-washed grind of purpose.
  Solitude

undertaken makes you lonelier
  than you expected; the sound of heat not
speaking *specifically* to you
  through the vents you thought was
music from another room,
  so you go stand in another

room, and no; nothing. Hard to not hear,
  like staring down a snowblare in association
with the fireball of the sun.
  In order to look through
the microscope
  the ornamental gilt finial

cap needs to be unscrewed.
  Which we never do. Never? No; never.
In fact a patrolling Design Assistant
  screws it harder
every time he passes. *In fact,*
  or in this poem? In the fact

of this poem in which I need to back up
  a few paces to specify
my mother just texted
  "Not a Dodge, a Chevy"

in response to what I asked her a few hours ago
    and should go back

and make a change to
    though dearly want I to say we got out of dodge
in regard to by-chance survival
    and now have done so thrice and so it stands.
Truth and lies and art
    are twisty business. The Art-

ful Dodger learned his
    from "The Jew" it humiliates me to read about
who was contrived on a desk of
    mahogany of Honduras, same wood
upon which, salvaged
    from a shipping container

at the port of Amsterdam—
    as he would years later
paint a bible scene
    of gang rape and murder
on panel reclaimed from an imported crate of sugar—
    Rembrandt created his first commissioned

portrait in 1631 and dated
    upside-down on a small
slip of paper
    in the subject's left hand,
a bit demonically to my eye,
    hanging bottoms-up like that like a bat at rest

rendered smoothly on paper
    on the very species of wood that reflects,
in the words of Dickens,
    in the depth of its grain,

through all its polish, the hue of the wretched who felled it.
    What is your desk

made of? I'm just
    writing on my lap right
now, upon which once I rocked my son
    in mothering blue silence that felt beyond
beyond, but these luxurious pants were ginned
    in Egypt of a cotton

subjected to the arbitrary wash
    of the Nile Delta, which in its distance
from where this Museum
    roots its Christmas tree,
this time of year makes for faster
    convoluting routing toward the

portrait of the ancestor, and so I backtrack
    the descendant
through the Sackler Wing of Ancient Egypt
    where last year Nan Goldin threw
hundreds of empty pill bottles
    prescribed to the donor the

dehydrated pill-bottle color of deathbed urine
    into water that stands
in the Museum
    for the banks of the Nile where the Temple
of Dendur rises
    on its dislocated slab. I

read Goldin's parents married
    the very day the Nazis
invaded Poland. History
    eyes union strangely back through her lens

lying in the bed of her self-portrait (not
    on view), *Nan*

and Brian in Bed, NYC,
    hanging in humming interior amber
a few years before Brian
    beat her so brutally her left eye
nearly came out of her head. Afterward,
    while she lay on

the floor unconscious, he used her bright red lipstick
    to write "Jewish American Princess"
on the mirror over the sink
    of their hotel room
in Berlin. Snapshots were not considered
    real art. The

anecdotes of art history,
    worse if a woman
takes them: gossip. "No people
    live longer than the documents
of their culture." Know who said that?
    Contemplate it a few cool beats while I look out my

window and watch a squirrel nibble an acorn,
    maybe fold some laundry, and talk to my son
if he answers his phone
    in the backseat of the car. Nick lowers
the radio because we're
    together on

the speaker now
    and I tell them
I love them, drive carefully, I'll be thinking of you. They're
    on their way home from a fencing tournament

in Myrtle Beach. My son took gold, beating
      all other twelve-year-olds,

even his teammates, but
      that's the sport. You practice together then
stab your best friend in the heart with
      the null blade of a real foil. It makes a mother proud
and ashamed. Do you ever
      confuse figure and

ground? The year Nan
      Goldin's parents married and the possibility of
her tormented gaze to make something of
      artificial moonlight
going down on the hood of a dirty car
      upon which a

friend is passed out
      entered the national stop bath
it was Hitler who said it,
      referring to a porcelain figurine of a fencer leaning
on his weapon, shirt off,
      porcelain flesh the white of his

porcelain pants, part
      of the uniform called in toto his "whites."
"White porcelain
      is the embodiment
of the German soul," he continued, took
      Poland, and also made the Meissen porcelain factory

the expressive tool of the Reich with satellite operation
      in Dachau by Dachau labor. Among
the miniature figures envisioned there,
      glazed, fired,

and ceremoniously
　　given

as gifts to loyalists,
　　the most terrifying is not
the handsome porcelain fencer soldier;
　　it's that soldier's shiny German shepherd,
giant ears alert
　　to the sound of something inexpressible.

Not on view, Goldin's photo of a real bruise
　　the shape of a painted-on heart.
You wouldn't believe the composition:
　　plotted on a disheveled grid
of cheap textiles, someone
　　pulling down her hose to

show a gorgeous
　　cordate bruise it hurts to see.
Healed before the film was even developed/
　　it will never heal.
Bruising in collusion with graffiti on
　　the face of that Temple—built 10-below

if years were weather: "Leonardo 1820"
　　eternalized with steady hand by the kind of man
who writes his name on
　　everything.
"Eternalized"
　　is premature. Imposed. Asserted. It

was the Ancient Egyptians
　　who introduced the branding iron
to the side of a cow; passed it to the Romans
　　who told themselves it was

for the protection of the spirit of
    the animal

that a spell was burned
    in flesh. Some to the Temple
travel in the name of Isis. Some
    to serve a pair of seated, recently
human brothers who backed
    the Romans against a kingdom invading

from the south.
    Strategic immortals,
one in stylized stone cobra headdress, other outdoing
    the first in matching cobra hood
further adorned by two upright ostrich feathers
    firm with grace that makes

them choice vehicles for
    deliverance
of the soul. I strove to diffuse
    into Aeolian sandstone such as this once, too
—a million million individual grains of sand
    winter windblown

up the stoss slope,
    across the brink, down the slip face,
and then fanned by summer breeze
    back again,
power-striping the deposit
    with elemental cross strata over unimaginable amounts

of hours, empires, intervals, and breaths
    forming a rippling curtain
of cross-bedding rock face
    that looks like it isn't flowing

but it is. If you could part that curtain
    like tragic velvet swinging

open at the theater,
    sheer at the bedroom window
looking down upon a yard
    no longer yours,
what couldn't you quarry? Time? Truth? Death? I tried to climb back
    into bed with you this morning but you said

you'd rather be alone. And so you are, as I
    am, too. Here comes Pharaoh who's
not Pharaoh; he's Caesar Augustus,
    emperor of Rome dressed in local regalia;
Caesar Augustus,
    emperor

of Rome,
    was never in this Temple but
was represented by a priest who did "Pharaoh's"
    work of honoring the Goddess.
A personification of spring comes
    with him to the altar bringing

chicks trembling in her basket. Fear
    for whoever plays Spring
fills the pavilion with nervous sunlight. Here
    giant staff luncheons were held by Brooke
Astor every year! Creamy
    chicken salad sandwiches

served on bread's answer
    to cotton candy. You came on your lunch hour
and sat wherever there was an open chair
    beside someone who was already

eating at ten-top banquet tables
    spread in

honor of staff appreciation,
    but felt like a disembodied wedding
where the bride
    is everyone and you're marrying
someone you've never met named
    Money who has no idea how to

enter you. Here comes the Design Assistant
    pulling up a chair with one hand
and balancing his plate of sandwiches
    with the other. Cocky
from his recent
    promotion from Museum guard he

mounts the chair backward
    in the manner a child arrives by
imaginary horse. I played a game
    called "train" with my sister on days
my mother moved the high-backed kitchen chairs
    into a row in a

nearby room so she
    could mop the kitchen floor.
Needs two players; all you do is sit down
    one behind the other and say nothing
until you pull up to the station
    at your imagination's stop.

My station is near and
    I am trained to await it patiently
until excusing myself with a finalizing
    disembarking nod and exit this

world. There is a beat
    called eternity

when the train stills before the automatic doors
    slide open during
which I make eye contact with
    a baby on the lap of his mother asleep
in a window seat overlooking
    the vast bled

Meadowlands of Hackensack where
    cockroaches breed in backwash
at the base of a beer can
    under a bridge. During our brief
staring contest baby
    downloads memory of beforelife into my

fear of death and vice
    versa. Confession:
yesterday I slipped a piece of my hair into
    an archival file
of information about the *Rembrandt/*
    Not Rembrandt exhibition I requested

from the Museum library. I wanted
    to be a bigger part of it
than just the girl who gave directions
    but now I have
misgivings. The face of exhibition
    and pamphlet cover boy

is *Portrait*
    of a Man ("The Auctioneer"). Across the brow
of the murky reproduction
    of the original, authentic fraudulent

painting by an artist only
    known now as Follower

of Rembrandt
    some curator's assistant's assistant
identified the internal department of origin
    by scrawling
European Paintings
    on the only place bright enough to use a

ballpoint pen in all that shadow,
    resonating in its placement with the horror
of the tattoo on Charles
    Manson's forehead, of which he said,
"The mark on my head simulates
    the dead head black stamp

of rejection . . . death, terror, fear." *The Auctioneer*
    was bequeathed
by B. Altman, father of modern retail
    and secret collector of "severe" portraits
of merchants and bankers
    of the Low Countries,

amassing them the way Frick collected
    pink countesses, your neighbor hides
something in the compartment
    in his attic floor he
doesn't know his son's friends
    know of, and—field entomologist first and

foremost who wrote, *If your collection*
    is larger, even a shade larger, than any other
like it in the world,
    that greatly increases your happiness—

Alfred Kinsey gathered
　　a million beautiful

individual wasp galls
　　to study under his lens.
Demotion from real
　　Rembrandt to Rembrandt
parasite was undertaken slowly by mean assessment of
　　several points of glaring weakness:

indiscernibly ghostly
　　bust of no
one in particular deep in green shadow
　　too far behind The Auctioneer; abrupt
divisions of light and dark that contradict
　　the burn of actual

sun fascinating
　　the surface of the mortal world,
its lichens and somber orchids,
　　knives and rats and oysters, the glowing
structural sheens of which, though undepicted,
　　are illuminated by

authenticity of intensity
　　in a better painting
of anything; and while there is a curtain here,
　　no care stirred in the viewer for what's behind it—
he could be
　　anywhere, same as

being nowhere,
　　another way of saying,
not being
　　at all. Of the competence nevertheless

clear in certain of The Follower's passages, the might-be
    of his sad eyes and the tattered

edge of ledger concerning something out of frame
    he clutches with his present hand that's as
softly burdened with uncanny
    humanity as the paw of
a raccoon, "authorship
    is defined by

intellectual conception,
    not manual labor." Caveat emptor, Benjamin
Altman, as applied to
    real estate, objects, art—
information asymmetry
    and monopolies on

knowledge notwithstanding.
    What's Latin for
"Beware the Buyer"? The Rembrandt
    Rembrandts in the room
were purchased and made gifts of by a third-generation
    sugar refining fortune of a New York

family who refined their slaughtercash
    in giddy buying trips
to Europe from whence it brought fine drawings,
    prints, sculptures, ceramics, fine glass,
metalwork, weapons, lacquerwork, Old Masters
    and new blood

back to America. An old
    tradition to wash money in fine art.
In a refinery of sugar
    sugar is refined

through ritual cleansing with stockyard bone
    ground like that charred at low

oxygen to create
    the bone black pigment
that paints living shadows behind each
    painted merchant and defines that figure's
jaw and collar, cloak and doublet. Somewhere
    in the afterlife of bovine,

resurrected,
    forthcoming skeletal
with Death astride, who'll ride anyone
    to get here, the bones that compose the paint
and the bones that bought those paintings
    repatriate in an apocalyptic

herd. Balzac wrote,
    Behind every great fortune
is a great crime. Behind every great
    hoard into which that fortune pools:
a slaughterhouse. Yes, I embedded
    there my strand of hair; and further confession:

recently my family
    had lice. (Too Much Information
Desk!) What if I passed lice to the
    Metropolitan Museum of Art? I'm assured this
is impossible yet just read
    amoebas

were able to solve a simulation
    of the maze at Hampton Court. What couldn't
lice do to merely survive
    cold storage in a vertical file

they didn't already pursue
    on the heads of kings? They're

doing it now; it's
    done and re-upping already
at the roots. I can live with the suck of lice
    if I don't think about exponential
multigenerational fucking so close
    to the seat

of thinking itself
    but can't stop this course
of thought. Crawling with life,
    I could not bring myself
even to look at a single louse engorged with my own
    blood the holy proprietor of Lice Clinics

of America tenderly withdrew with tweezers from
    a fine-tooth metal comb he'd
just run through my hair
    and placed alive under
the lens of the hobby microscope
    he and his wife keep in the

clinic attached to their house
    in which, when his wife came through
a swinging interior door
    pulling on her rubber gloves, I saw
a long couch of judgmental daughters
    watching TV with their hair pulled

back so tight it made my eyes
    water. If there is
a God
    God loves lice and onto the food chain

situated them at the apex
    with the filthy forceps of his vectoring lips that kiss every

face of earth, passer-of-pestilence
    beast by suffering beast
the source of the infection of which
    is the contamination
of creation. I refused
    to see the bloated louse. Would not lean my

curiosity down into that eyepiece
    to meet what I fed
and immediately a swirling shame
    I recognized from earlier
refusal of knowledge
    married regret in my gut. Sounds

like I made it up: when I was fifteen
    David Copperfield came to my hometown,
where he'd also
    grown up. Came back
from his fame to play
    a fundraiser in our high school auditorium for a

dying friend. Dying then;
    long dead
now. There was to be a volunteer
    preordained to be chosen at random from
the audience whom David Copperfield
    would levitate in the finale. He

charged his favorite former teacher/
    my favored English teacher then with preselecting
a local to raise her hand to be
    called upon by chance to take the stage.

We were reading *Great*
    Expectations in

class. Love, dust, redemption,
    fate, choice, imperialism, and
lace. Magic doesn't ask twice, and having
    denied stagecraft and liftoff
the weight of my body,
    in awe and anger at myself I watched

a classmate rise and hover
    as the magician passed her
through a Hula-Hoop to prove
    there were no strings. I was backstage. A stagehand. I
could feel gravity
    making lemonade, in love with dirt and

time and concrete, dropping pennies off
    the Empire State Building and lying down
in new grass damp beside
    the reclining bodies it debases,
but everything wants
    to ascend. This was a few years

after David Copperfield
    disappeared the Statue of
Liberty on TV, concluding, ". . . I thought if we
    faced the emptiness . . ."
Asked to respond to monumental absence
    a white guy in the

live audience nods his closed face and says, "When
    the curtain went up and there was nothing there
I just couldn't believe it."
    What

was   it   I   was   saying
    about the infestation I introduced to

the Museum when I interrupted myself
    with magical thinking?
A lice comb, not on view, fabricated
    of tortoiseshell
attests there is art also
    in hell, much of it useful and small; you

can still pick imperial
    St. Petersburg from its fine teeth. The opposite
of a Fabergé egg,
    eggs are embedded in it
as in an ovary and belongs in this
    wasted period

room of my youth but there isn't space for everything
    and day distorts some items
the way it walks sleeping vampires
    into the dawn. I'll descend
into subbasement storage
    and deaccession it

safe in my clerkish bun
    up through the Department of Arms and Armor, an
engine room fixed between Egypt,
    Europe, and America,
where indirect light
    will speak softly of

time to it with
    a rapier's blade
and watch me style my electric hair in the blade's thin mirror,
    unloosing upon the new world

old nits. Arms and the man-
    made hammered steel plate carapace inspired

by the exoskeleton of the roach; arms and
    the mansion
you can stroll through the Neoclassical-
    United-States-Branch-Bank facade of which
and sit your imagination
    down in a scroll-back

dining chair that looks like
    the Articles of Confederation as if dreamed up
by a sofa, and feast there in mind
    on Federalist crow overlooking
Central Park. What   do   I
    know   of

the   dreams   of   things?   Lying together in
    darkness last night Nick told me he sort of
believes we live in a
    computer simulation. I live in
my poems, I said, which is
    another way of

asking him to stop talking
    about the whirl
of the computer fan heavy breathing
    under our Ikea bed. But how to exit
the Museum? Each day
    during the final ten minutes the

Museum is open the army of Museum guards
    surfaces from within the maze,
creeping around statuary and
    columns and inches in

slow motion down the Great Steps
    in formation

using the polar-magnetic
    push of their uniformed bodies
to repel visitors from the galleries
    in a closing-time sweep. They stream from
all directions into
    the Great Hall down every

pillaged-earth corridor of goods
    hammered, blessed, blown, ground, dyed,
smuggled, lacquered, carved, painted, threaded,
    sold, stolen, polished, given,
and cursed, and hold themselves there in a circle
    around the Information

Desk until every visitor's gone and the locked
    doors deadbolted again. Like the Rockettes,
my boss said the first day
    I worked the Desk. They circled us.
He said they'll dance a kick-line now
    before clocking

out and I believed him
    and thus I remember them
dancing. I remember
    anticipating the dance, and the high kicks I imagined
I remember because I
    anticipated with my

eyes they were in perfect formation kicking,
    my whole soul against the glass
behind which the next moment is and the past
    where they would and would have danced.

But of course they would not; and did not;
and still are.

NOTES AND ACKNOWLEDGMENTS

I began working at the Information Desk in the Great Hall at the Metropolitan Museum of Art shortly after graduating from college. Intermittently between the cracks in my graduate school education during the few years following that, and then again when I returned to New York City as a young poet, I was generously welcomed back to the Desk no matter how far away I'd gone or for how long, subsequently assuming other roles in the Visitor Services Department and elsewhere in the Museum before regretfully moving out of the building on to other employment. My coming of age as an artist was inextricable from my intimate experience working in that Museum among its gorgeous, harrowing hoard that collides in time and space, where magic and mundane objects with and without auras awed me on my way to see portraits of heiresses whose families bought and sold the world. My time there amounted to a relatively short period of my life; it lasted forever. Though I haven't worked inside the Information Desk now for more than twenty years, the experience has so asserted itself into my art that I regard the Information Desk as my private writing desk; I am always seated there.

Some of the art, including literature, I come across in the course of the passages of *Information Desk: An Epic* is clearly identified in situ, and some of it is only silently acknowledged in passing. Here is as complete a list as I can draw, in order of appearance, of artworks that materialize within this book, though I salute all the works I encountered en route from here to there and back and which come to me in dreams sometimes in other inscrutable forms, the artists who created them, and the laborers responsible for harvesting the material, often in brutal circumstances, that makes making possible:

PART 1

Auguste Rodin, *Monument to Balzac*. Musée Rodin, Paris.

Philip Roth, *Portnoy's Complaint*. New York: Random House, 1969.

Edward J. Steichen, *Balzac, The Silhouette—4 A.M.*, 1908. The Metropolitan Museum of Art, New York.

Alexander Calder, *Mobile*, 1941. The Metropolitan Museum of Art, New York.

Unknown goldsmith, Wreath, 350–300 BCE. British Museum, London.

Auguste Rodin, *Final Study for the Monument to Balzac*, modeled 1897, cast 1972. The Metropolitan Museum of Art, New York.

Auguste Rodin, *Portrait of Balzac*, modeled 1893, cast 1926/1933. Art Institute of Chicago.

Honoré de Balzac, *Lily of the Valley*. New York: Carroll & Graf, 1989.

Phidias (?), Parthenon sculptures, ca. 5th century BCE. British Museum, London.

Unknown laborers, Obelisk of Thutmose III, known as "Cleopatra's Needle." Central Park, New York.

Unknown artist, Model of the Parthenon. Cast Collection, The Metropolitan Museum of Art, New York.

Unknown laborers, Temple of Dendur, ca. 10 BCE. The Metropolitan Museum of Art, New York.

Louis Henry Sullivan and Dankmar Adler, Staircase from Chicago Stock Exchange Building, 1893. The Metropolitan Museum of Art, New York.

Maira and Alex Kalman, *Sara Berman's Closet*, 2017. The Metropolitan Museum of Art, New York.

John Milton, *Paradise Lost*. London: Printed by S. Simmons, and to be sold by T. Helder, at the Angel in Little Brittain, 1669.

Follower of Rembrandt, *Portrait of a Man ("The Auctioneer")*, ca. 1658–1662. The Metropolitan Museum of Art, New York.

Unknown artists, for the rock-cut tomb of the royal chief steward Meketre, Model of a traveling boat being rowed, ca. 1981–1975 BCE, Middle Kingdom, Dynasty 12. The Metropolitan Museum of Art, New York.

Unknown artists, for the rock-cut tomb of the royal chief steward Meketre, Model of a porch and garden, ca. 1981–1975 BCE, Middle Kingdom, Dynasty 12. The Metropolitan Museum of Art, New York.

Unknown artists, for the rock-cut tomb of the royal chief steward Meketre, Model of a slaughterhouse, ca. 1981–1975 BCE, Middle Kingdom, Dynasty 12. The Metropolitan Museum of Art, New York.

Unknown artists, for the rock-cut tomb of the royal chief steward Meketre, Model of a cattle stable, ca. 1981–1975 BCE, Middle Kingdom, Dynasty 12. The Metropolitan Museum of Art, New York.

Unknown artists, for the rock-cut tomb of the royal chief steward Meketre, Model of a granary with scribes, ca. 1981–1975 BCE, Middle Kingdom, Dynasty 12. The Metropolitan Museum of Art, New York.

Unknown goldsmith, Gold solidus of Theodosius I, 379–395. The Metropolitan Museum of Art, New York.

Unknown artist, Glass weight, 6th–early 7th century. The Metropolitan Museum of Art, New York.

Emanuel Leutze, *Washington Crossing the Delaware*, 1851. The Metropolitan Museum of Art, New York.

Various unknown craftspeople, Room from the Hart House, Ipswich, Massachusetts, 1680. The Metropolitan Museum of Art, New York.

Charles Dickens, *Bleak House*. London: Bradbury and Evans, 1853.

Rosemary's Baby. Directed by Roman Polanski, performance by Mia Farrow. William Castle Productions, 1968.

June Jordan, *Passion: New Poems, 1977–1980*. Boston: Beacon Press, 1980.

House of Carl Fabergé, workmaster Henrik Emanuel Wigström, miniatures by Vassily Ivanovich Zuiev, Imperial Napoleonic egg, 1912. The Metropolitan Museum of Art, New York.

Elizabeth Bishop, *North & South*. Boston: Houghton Mifflin, 1946.

William Wordsworth, *The Prelude, or Growth of a Poet's Mind: An Autobiographical Poem*. London: Edward Moxon, 1850.

Eudora Welty, *Delta Wedding*. New York: Harcourt, Brace, 1946.

Winslow Homer, *Snap the Whip*, 1872. The Metropolitan Museum of Art, New York.

Unknown artist, Chess set, attributed to Iran, Nishapur, 12th century. The Metropolitan Museum of Art, New York.

PART 2

Lorenzo Bartolini, The Demidoff Table, 1845. The Metropolitan Museum of Art, New York.

Hiroshi Sugimoto, *Boden Sea, Uttwil*, 1993. The Metropolitan Museum of Art, New York.

Gustave Le Gray, [*The Great Wave, Sète*], 1857. The Metropolitan Museum of Art, New York.

Rembrandt van Rijn, *Girl at a Window*, 1645. Dulwich Picture Gallery, London.

Rembrandt van Rijn, *Le Boeuf écorché*, 1655. Louvre, Paris.

Rembrandt van Rijn, *Isaac and Rebecca*, known as *"The Jewish Bride,"* ca. 1655–ca. 1669. Rijksmuseum, Amsterdam.

Unknown craftspeople, Lower part of the door of a tomb, ca. 2051–1981 BCE. The Metropolitan Museum of Art, New York.

Lange de Bourbon (clockmaker) and Antoine-Nicolas Martinière (enameler), Wall clock-barometer, ca. 1770. The Metropolitan Museum of Art, New York.

Jean-Henri Riesener, Mechanical table, 1781. The Metropolitan Museum of Art, New York.

PART 3

Gilles Joubert, Writing table, 1759. The Metropolitan Museum of Art, New York.

"I S," Chamber candlestick, first half of 18th century. The Metropolitan Museum of Art, New York.

Follower of Rembrandt, Formerly known as *Christ with a Staff*, ca. 1660s. The Metropolitan Museum of Art, New York.

Jean-Auguste-Dominique Ingres, *Joséphine-Éléonore-Marie-Pauline de Galard de Brassac de Béarn (1825–1860), Princesse de Broglie*, 1851–1853. The Metropolitan Museum of Art, New York.

Jean-Auguste-Dominique Ingres, *Nude Study for a Portrait of Princesse de Broglie*, ca. 1852. Musée Bonnat-Helleu, Bayonne, France.

Attributed to Rafal Amezúa, *Choir Screen from the Cathedral of Valladolid*, ca. 1763. The Metropolitan Museum of Art, New York.

Unknown artist, *Crib of the Infant Jesus*, ca. 15th century. The Metropolitan Museum of Art, New York.

Claude-Siméon Passemant, Microscope, ca. 1750. The Metropolitan Museum of Art, New York.

Rembrandt van Rijn, *Nicolaes Ruts*, 1631. The Frick Collection, New York.

Charles Dickens and Wilkie Collins, *The Lazy Tour of Two Idle Apprentices*. London: Chapman and Hall, 1890.

Nan Goldin, *Nan and Brian in Bed, NYC*, 1983. The Metropolitan Museum of Art, New York.

Nan Goldin, *French Chris on the Convertible, NYC*, 1979. The Metropolitan Museum of Art, New York.

Ottmar Obermaier and unnamed artists at Dachau concentration camp for Porzellan Manufaktur Allach, *The Fencer*, 1938. Locations unknown.

Nan Goldin, *Heart-Shaped Bruise, NYC,* 1980. The Metropolitan Museum of Art, New York.

Photograph of Rembrandt/Not Rembrandt *Pamphlet,* 2019. Author's collection.

Charles Dickens, *Great Expectations.* London: Chapman and Hall, 1861.

Nicholls & Plincke, Lice comb (part of a set), 1848–1849. The Metropolitan Museum of Art, New York.

Unknown swordsmith, Rapier, Italian, ca. 1540. The Metropolitan Museum of Art, New York.

Unknown metalsmith, Shield of Henry II of France, ca. 1555. The Metropolitan Museum of Art, New York.

Martin Euclid Thompson (architect), Facade of the Second Branch Bank of the United States, 1822–1824. The Metropolitan Museum of Art, New York.

Many sources helped clarify and complicate my recollection of the collections. Those that indelibly influence how I think about or describe art, or most significantly illuminate the context of art objects, and whose presences surface most palpably in the passages of *Information Desk,* are these, cited here upon first sighting:

1   **When the American cockroach lands:** Christie Wilcox, *Venomous: How Earth's Deadliest Creatures Mastered Biochemistry* (New York: Scientific American/Farrar, Straus and Giroux, 2016).

17   Human consciousness far // predates me / oiling the mahogany handrail / with my mere presence: Jennifer L. Anderson, *Mahogany: The Costs of Luxury in Early America* (Cambridge, MA: Harvard University Press, 2012).

17   *Rembrandt/ / Not Rembrandt, / 1995, was the first special exhibition / I attended as Museum // employee:* Hubert von Sonnenburg, *Rembrandt/Not Rembrandt in the Metropolitan Museum of Art: Aspects of Connoisseurship*, vol. 1: *Paintings: Problems and Issues* (New York: Metropolitan Museum of Art, 1996).

17   without that indecisive // human "Or" Milton imposes: Peter C. Herman, "'Paradise Lost,' the Miltonic 'Or,' and the Poetics of Incertitude," *Studies in English Literature 1500–1900* 43, no. 1 (Winter 2003), 181–211.

18   "The handling / of the built-up impasto / is itself a valid argument / against": Walter Liedtke et al., *Rembrandt/Not Rembrandt in the Metropolitan Museum of Art: Aspects of Connoisseurship*, vol. 2: *Paintings, Drawings, and Prints: Art-Historical Perspectives* (New York: Metropolitan Museum of Art, 1996).

24   Afterward I'd tuck that Stoic / in eighty yards of wine-dark imported / European textile: Amelia Peck et al., *Period Rooms in the Metropolitan Museum of Art* (New York: Metropolitan Museum of Art, 1996).

28   detonating "in circumstances // beyond / the limits of acceptable fiction": John B. West, "Krook's Death by Spontaneous Combustion and the Controversy between Dickens and Lewes: A Physiologist's View," *The Dickensian* 90, no. 433 (Summer 1994), 125–29. Gordon S. Haight, "Dickens and Lewes on Spontaneous Combustion," *Nineteenth-Century Fiction* 10, no. 1 (June 1955), 53–63.

37   Something like a wooden pearl, what gall / forms here: Eric R. Eaton, *Wasps: The Astonishing Diversity of a Misunderstood Insect* (Princeton, NJ: Princeton University Press, 2021).

45–46 they could only reach by // locating first a marble table, / once listed lost / on an inventory in Italy: Deborah Menaker, "Lorenzo Bartolini's Demidoff Table," *Metropolitan Museum Journal* 17 (1982), 75–86.

46   "a curious revelation of *ennui*": James Jackson Jarves, "Prince Demidoff's Sale: Preparing to Disperse a Great Art Collection, the Result of Enormous Wealth and Untrained Taste," *The New York Times*, February 1, 1880.

46 **"My dear // General"** and **"I shall be happy to":** Menaker, "Lorenzo Bartolini's Demidoff Table."

46 **rank the director / claimed "without any supporting evidence":** Michael Gross, *Rogues' Gallery: The Secret Story of the Lust, Lies, Greed, and Betrayals That Made the Metropolitan Museum of Art* (New York: Broadway Books, 2009).

53 **From the vacancy comes tromping / the grunting, // lowing frequency of the hand-ground, / hoof-mouth pigment "bone black":** David Coles, *Chromatopia: An Illustrated History of Color* (New York: Thames & Hudson, 2019).

57 **reds are the // most forsaken:** Amy Butler Greenfield, *A Perfect Red: Empire, Espionage, and the Quest for the Color of Desire* (New York: HarperCollins, 2005).

63 **The detection / of life in art / is serious:** R. J. Koestler, "Detecting and Controlling Insect Infestation in Fine Art," in *Pacific 2000: Proceedings of the 5th International Conference on Easter Island and the Pacific*, ed. C. M. Stevenson, G. Lee, and F. J. Morin (Los Osos, CA: Easter Island Foundation), 541–45.

79 **brought by coat pocket into / a French period room where the Trustees were / gathered for dinner behind a // folding screen, / cockroaches landed DOA in proximity / to the writing desk of Louis XV:** Julia Bryan-Wilson, *Art Workers: Radical Practice in the Vietnam War Era* (Berkeley: University of California Press, 2009).

81 **In the season of the cockroach / someone made his mark by blade:** Bridget R. Cooks, "Black Artists and Activism: *Harlem on My Mind* (1969)," *American Studies* 48, no. 1 (Spring 2007), 5–39. Martin Arnold, "Paintings Defaced at Metropolitan; One a Rembrandt," *The New York Times*, January 17, 1969.

85 **quickly on / the runway with mud she / rolled into a globe and // flew here from a nearby puddle, / a keyhole wasp / sculpts her secret nest:** Alan P. N. House, "Insects and Aviation Safety: The Case of the Keyhole Wasp *Pachodynerus nasidens* (Hymenoptera: Vespidae) in Australia," *Transportation Research Interdisciplinary Perspectives* 4 (February 2020), 100096.

92 **Churchill called anecdotes / *the gleaming toys of history*:** Mark Campbell, "The Gleaming Toys," in *Dirt*, ed. Megan Born, Helene Furján, and Lily Jelks, with Philip M. Crosby (Philadelphia: PennDesign; Cambridge, MA: MIT Press, 2012), 36–39. Here Churchill is alluding to Dr. Johnson, as was wisely pointed out to me in the copyediting phase of this book by a production editor at Penguin.

97   I // read Goldin's parents married / the very day the Nazis / invaded Poland: Hilton Als, "Dark Rooms," *The New Yorker*, July 4, 2016.

"Hyman and Lillian met in Boston and married on September 1, 1939, the day Germany invaded Poland."

99   referring to a porcelain figurine of a fencer leaning / on his weapon, shirt off, / porcelain flesh the white of his // porcelain pants: Edmund de Waal, *The White Road: Journey into an Obsession* (New York: Picador, 2015).

I am indebted to this whole extraordinary book, but especially to chapter 60, "what whiteness, what candor," in which de Waal reveals, "The most desired of all these figures was a muscled youth, shirtless, leaning on his epée, *Die Fechter*, The Fencer. It was given only to the elite in the party" (354). Two paragraphs later he translates a passage from an SS news source quoting Hitler in 1939: "No people live longer than the document of their culture." And quoting "the first catalogue for Allach": "White porcelain is the embodiment of the German soul" (356).

105   father of modern retail / and secret collector of "severe" portraits / of merchants and bankers / of the Low Countries: Francis Haskell, "The Benjamin Altman Bequest," *Metropolitan Museum Journal* 3 (1970), 259–80.

107   "authorship / is defined by // intellectual conception, / not manual labor": Michael FitzGerald, "Really Rembrandt," *Vogue*, October 1995.

Grateful acknowledgment is made to the staff and poetry editors (Brian Blanchfield, Ben Lerner, Paul Muldoon, Meghan O'Rourke, and Paisley Rekdal) of the following publications where excerpts from *Information Desk: An Epic* were previously published: the Poem-a-Day feature of the Academy of American Poets, *Harper's*, *The New Yorker*, *The Yale Review*, and *The Best American Poetry 2020* (Simon & Schuster).

I am enormously thankful for the sanctuaries of the Corporation of Yaddo, MacDowell, and the Joseph Brodsky Rome Prize, a gift of the Drue Heinz Trust, at the American Academy in Rome. I am also grateful for the support of Emory University, and my coven there.

Gratitude to Han VanderHart, who nonchalantly dropped the term "the Miltonic 'Or'" in workshop one day at the Iowa Summer Writing Festival and changed the course of this poem. Thank you, Paul Slovak, for your commitment to poetry and your golden patience. Profound appreciation to my old friends at the Met, wherever you are. My warmest, loving gratitude to Nick and Sacha, who are my life. Nick coined the brilliant term "murderwealth" and granted me permission to save it for a rainy day, which this is. Additionally, I acknowledge learning from and remixing language and information that appears on the Met's website.

And finally, this book is dedicated to David, Suzanne, and Eula, who every morning, in a season of doom, met me for poetry: thank you, dear friends.

© Nicole Craine

Robyn Schiff is the author of three previous collections of poetry: *Worth*, *Revolver*, and *A Woman of Property*, which was a finalist for the Los Angeles Times Book Prize. Schiff's poems have appeared in *The New Yorker*, *The New Republic*, *The American Poetry Review*, *The Yale Review*, *Poetry*, and elsewhere. The recipient of the Joseph Brodsky Rome Prize in Literature, she is a professor at the University of Chicago and coedits Canarium Books.

GAROUS
ABDOLMALEKIAN
Lean Against This Late Hour

PAIGE ACKERSON-KIELY
Dolefully, A Rampart Stands

JOHN ASHBERY
Selected Poems
Self-Portrait in a Convex
   Mirror

PAUL BEATTY
Joker, Joker, Deuce

JOSHUA BENNETT
Owed
The Sobbing School
The Study of Human Life

TED BERRIGAN
The Sonnets

LAUREN BERRY
The Lifting Dress

JOE BONOMO
Installations

PHILIP BOOTH
Lifelines: Selected Poems
   1950–1999
Selves

JIM CARROLL
Fear of Dreaming:
   The Selected Poems
Living at the Movies
Void of Course

SU CHO
The Symmetry of Fish

RIO CORTEZ
Golden Ax

ALISON HAWTHORNE
DEMING
Genius Loci
Rope
Stairway to Heaven

CARL DENNIS
Another Reason
Callings
Earthborn
New and Selected Poems
   1974–2004
Night School
Practical Gods
Ranking the Wishes
Unknown Friends

DIANE DI PRIMA
Loba

STUART DISCHELL
Backwards Days
Dig Safe

STEPHEN DOBYNS
Velocities: New and Selected
   Poems 1966–1992

EDWARD DORN
Way More West

HEID E. ERDRICH
Little Big Bully

ROGER FANNING
The Middle Ages

ADAM FOULDS
The Broken Word: An Epic
   Poem of the British Empire
   in Kenya, and the Mau Mau
   Uprising Against It

CARRIE FOUNTAIN
Burn Lake
Instant Winner
The Life

AMY GERSTLER
Dearest Creature
Ghost Girl
Index of Women
Medicine
Nerve Storm
Scattered at Sea

EUGENE GLORIA
Drivers at the Short-Time Motel
Hoodlum Birds
My Favorite Warlord
Sightseer in This Killing City

DEBORA GREGER
In Darwin's Room

ZEINA HASHEM BECK
O

TERRANCE HAYES
American Sonnets for My Past
   and Future Assassin
Hip Logic
How to Be Drawn
Lighthead
So to Speak
Wind in a Box

NATHAN HOKS
The Narrow Circle

ROBERT HUNTER
Sentinel and Other Poems

MARY KARR
Viper Rum

WILLIAM KECKLER
Sanskrit of the Body

JACK KEROUAC
Book of Blues
Book of Haikus
Book of Sketches

JOANNA KLINK
Circadian
Excerpts from a Secret
   Prophecy
The Nightfields
Raptus

JOANNE KYGER
As Ever: Selected Poems

ANN LAUTERBACH
Door
Hum
If in Time: Selected Poems
   1975–2000
On a Stair
Or to Begin Again
Spell
Under the Sign

CORINNE LEE
Plenty
Pyx

PENGUIN POETS

PHILLIS LEVIN
May Day
Mercury
Mr. Memory & Other Poems

PATRICIA LOCKWOOD
Motherland Fatherland
  Homelandsexuals

WILLIAM LOGAN
Rift of Light

J. MICHAEL MARTINEZ
Museum of the Americas

ADRIAN MATEJKA
The Big Smoke
Map to the Stars
Mixology
Somebody Else Sold the World

MICHAEL McCLURE
Huge Dreams: San Francisco
  and Beat Poems

ROSE McLARNEY
Forage
Its Day Being Gone

DAVID MELTZER
David's Copy: The Selected
  Poems of David Meltzer

TERESA K. MILLER
Borderline Fortune

ROBERT MORGAN
Dark Energy
Terroir

CAROL MUSKE-DUKES
Blue Rose
An Octave Above Thunder:
  New and Selected Poems
Red Trousseau
Twin Cities

ALICE NOTLEY
Certain Magical Acts
Culture of One
The Descent of Alette
Disobedience
For the Ride
In the Pines
Mysteries of Small Houses

WILLIE PERDOMO
The Crazy Bunch
The Essential Hits of Shorty
  Bon Bon

DANIEL POPPICK
Fear of Description

LIA PURPURA
It Shouldn't Have Been
  Beautiful

LAWRENCE RAAB
The History of Forgetting

BARBARA RAS
The Last Skin
One Hidden Stuff

MICHAEL ROBBINS
Alien vs. Predator
The Second Sex
Walkman

PATTIANN ROGERS
Flickering
Generations
Holy Heathen Rhapsody
Quickening Fields
Wayfare

SAM SAX
Madness

ROBYN SCHIFF
Information Desk
A Woman of Property

WILLIAM STOBB
Absentia
Nervous Systems

TRYFON TOLIDES
An Almost Pure Empty
  Walking

VINCENT TORO
Tertulia

PAUL TRAN
All the Flowers Kneeling

SARAH VAP
Viability

ANNE WALDMAN
Gossamurmur
Kill or Cure
Manatee/Humanity
Trickster Feminism

JAMES WELCH
Riding the Earthboy 40

PHILIP WHALEN
Overtime: Selected Poems

PHILLIP B. WILLIAMS
Mutiny

ROBERT WRIGLEY
Anatomy of Melancholy and
  Other Poems
Beautiful Country
Box
Earthly Meditations:
  New and Selected Poems
Lives of the Animals
Reign of Snakes
The True Account of Myself
  as a Bird

MARK YAKICH
The Importance of Peeling
  Potatoes in Ukraine
Spiritual Exercises
Unrelated Individuals Forming
  a Group Waiting to Cross